Edward Ryder

The Morning Star

A poem

Edward Ryder

The Morning Star
A poem

ISBN/EAN: 9783337037840

Printed in Europe, USA, Canada, Australia, Japan

Cover: Foto ©Thomas Meinert / pixelio.de

More available books at **www.hansebooks.com**

THE MORNING STAR.

A POEM

BY

EDWARD RYDER

NEW YORK
PUBLISHED FOR THE AUTHOR BY
G. P. PUTNAM'S SONS
182 Fifth Avenue
1878

THE MORNING STAR.

I.

AS a Pomologist his Nursery
   Of thorny seedlings with judicious eye
Surveys, electing one whereon to graft
Some choice Exotic, strait, with knife or saw,
Close to the ground, severs the polished stem
And lays the native crown with all its buds
To wither like life's morning dreams, anon
Splits the complaining stump and there inserts
A Scion, severed from its native tree
And clime, but holding fast its proper life,
Closes with balm the wounds, and bids the root
Regenerate, so from destruction saved,
Transmute its spirituous energies to feed
The renovating germ, till, in due time,
In steadfast wedlock knit, the double tree,
Spreading new leaf and bloom, unto the hand

Of its approving lord the golden fruit
Tenders, most pleasing to his taste—so God
This sour, degenerate World grafted with Christ.
From many nations one of purest root
He chose, (from worlds perhaps the one most fair
And meet to be the womb of spirit life
That should flow forth and people sister orbs,)
Nourished it long, pruned it with patient care,
And as hope's fairest buds began to swell,
Smote off with Roman sword its native crown,
And in the bleeding stock of empire set
The Branch of Life's immortal Tree in Heaven.
Ere long the Gospel Scion spread abroad
In twelve coördinate limbs which, with new shoots
Adorned, like honorable setting found
Upon the savage nations, thus from clime
To clime expanding and yet more to spread,
Until the ransomed Earth, blushing at last
With tints of Paradise, shall offer up,
On all her friendly interlacing boughs,
The fruit of Perfect Manhood unto God.

All men are units of one greater Man,
Mankind,—the sentient corpuscles that form
The mystic body of Humanity.
They are the leaves which rustle on Time's boughs,
Flung off as generations fade. But lo!
Not all the leaf decays; the better part,
If summer were not idly spent, remains,
In frost-defying buds whose vital store

The industrious leaf all summer has laid by,
From sun and earth and the soft-breathing winds,
To form a branch of life's interior frame.

He that has read the story of a leaf
Has read the story of the Oak, and found
The golden key to Wisdom's treasury,
Strong to unlock the deep vaults of the Past
And put his wealth to use, while, at a turn,
It opens the vast manufactory
In which the busy Present weaves the robes
Of her dear child, the ever unborn Future.
Experience is the alphabet of thought;
It is the telescope through which we view
E'en Heaven, and with its kindred lights converse.
But think not, when thy glass reveals no more,
There is Truth's bound : wait till another lens
Be given thee, larger, more polished ; nay,
Add lens to lens, each broader than the last,
Till Herschel's world-creating tube shall seem
A straw, and yet will Truth show nebulous front.
So to Experience add Hope, nor deem
God's works distorted if thy glass be rough,
Nor that thy flickering taper can reveal
Life's mysteries without that heavenly Ray,
Which only can illuminate the page
Of thy brief history, or that, more large,
Of which it forms a part, the ample scroll
Of a World's chronicles, itself too small
For the Great Teacher's words—itself a page

Of the illimitable Volume where,
With pen and brush dipped in celestial dyes,
Heaven's peerless Artist labors to portray
The face of God's colossal loveliness,
Still ever breaking in more glorious smiles.

Good men are the Great Poet's capitals;
Each life a line of Earth's grand Epic. Some,
Though harsh and tuneless to man's ear, contain
More poesy than human wit ere wrought
Into the texture of its noblest songs.
Some are historic, some didactic, some
Laden with prophecy. Full many end
With exclamations, questions, or a dash;—
Most have a comma, but some glide right on
Against the margin as if one brief line
Could ill-express the meaning of a life.

What to an angel's eye is human state,
And the soul of man that hasteth thus away?
A dew-drop on a trembling blade of grass,
Or blushing petal, poised so tenderly
That a fly's wing may brush it to the ground:
Yet in its tiny orb all nature's wealth
And beauty are reflected, till it seems
Itself a universe. From Heaven's warm breast
On the soft lap of slumbering Earth distilled,
In dreams and wonderment the live-long night
It muses on the various face of being,
To honor, wealth or fame, which like the moon

And stars adorn its heavens, brief homage pays,
Till the ascending Sun obscures their beams,
When, fixing on its Lord adoring eyes,
It flames with Love, impatient to be free,
And melting spreads its viewless wings for Heaven.

In such a mirror, orbing gracefully
On a fair petal of the seven-leaved rose,
Our mother spread around her bounteous heart.
Has heavenly Wisdom such instruction lent
To my admiring eyes, that my fond muse,
Somewhat by partial tenderness inspired,
But zealous chiefly that a sighing World
And a disheveled Church may learn the way
To Unity and Peace, and fall in love
With Love and Charity, would fain invoke
The presence of these self-same wings of God,
To brood above her and indite a song
For Time's last days, fit for the gathering choirs
To sing in that Broad Temple unto which
The nations now are hastening, Her first fruits
Thus consecrated, He whose breath alone
Can blow our hopes to port, may deign a smile,
And bid salvation or instruction wait
Upon his humble messenger. So blessed,
Two angels fair shall steal through all the land,
And in its parlors and in its cabins cry,
"Sweet friends, the Lord has sent to bid you come
And make his arms your home : wash you therefore,
And take upon you love's white, bridal robe,

And crown your foreheads with the Morning Star,
And come—lo, He is even at the door!"

Think you Heaven slept when the sly sorcerer charmed
The ear of Eve and made her breast the grave
Of Innocence and Joy, turning her forth
From ease and affluence to till her soul
In poverty and strife, for one good fruit
Bringing forth many empty, vain conceits,
Gendered abundantly, with travail pain,
To fill the earth with violence and woe?
Why did not all the angels shout alarm,
And break the bold seducer's magic spell?
Seemed it a little thing, to Him who built
Man for eternity, that he should spend
A day in strife, tumbling and sighs, to learn
What foes infest the road to happiness,
Perhaps to this rude cradle unconfined?
A little thing, to Love omnipotent,
To recreate a blighted heart or world?
A little thing, that billions should go out
In darkness, who might else have ever lived
Like white-robed infants in the lap of ease?
Or, if these things be great, were it more sad
That man should never rise the goodly heights
Of moral excellence and taste the joys
Of liberty and virtue, without which
He were but a more intellectual ape?—
And still we ask, O warning angel, why
Thou dost but whisper while temptation roars?

Why hides the light of wisdom in the grave
Before it takes the empire of the soul?
—So we were all dumb watch-dogs, not one barked
When that sly thief Ambition stole at morn
To our Elysian fold, and with his gloss
Beguiled our happy Nymph to grasp the boughs
Of Knowledge with such idolizing greed
As broke great Nature's law, and on her head,
Instead of myrtle wreaths, an iron crown
Implanted; so from learning's paradise
She sadly turned away, and that more fair
Of ruddy and elastic health, to search
Through desolated Eden for some balm
That could avert the fiery sword of pain,
Which kept the ways of knowledge from her feet.

Thus Nature's beauteous crown was laid in dust.
Long it refused to die, by hope sustained,
Till in its stead at length a fairer rose,
Lifting toward Heaven its fragrant leaf and bloom,
In holier aspiration. O how sweet
Is the returning Sun when midnight storms
Have drenched the vale in tears, when drooping flowers
Hang on their broken stalks, trying to smile
In their humility! As the warm beams
Dispel the mists and change the pendant drops
To glittering diamonds, tree, shrub, and flower
Seem vocal with angelic melodies,
Hymning the wonders of Redeeming Love,
Which out of darkness still reveals new light,

Life in the midst of death,—mourning transforms
To praise, and bondage into liberty!

Behold the Fugitive from sin's dark thrall,
Long by the World enslaved, whose profitless
And rigid yoke God's hand at length has loosed,
By judgments and afflictions manifold
On the self-seeking and rebellious Heart
Oft melted in the furnace of God's wrath,
But presently as hard as penitent snow
After the sun goes down. Fast through the depths
Of Judgment's roaring sea, asunder cleft
By faith's potential Rod, his narrow path
The Pilgrim flies, pursued by Satan's hosts
And sheltered by the intervening arm
Of God's paternal providence, which sheds
Light on his pathway, but upon his foes
Disaster and confusion! Safe at length
On mercy's banks, like one through death escaped
The pains and perils of this stormy clime,
Backward he casts a happy glance to see
The World and all its tinsel overwhelmed
In that baptismal gulf. Exultant then,
He sows the shore with melody and praise!

A needful sabbath spent, wherein he feasts
On the unleavened bread of charity,
With water from salvation's living wells,
And just before him sees Heaven's open door,
God leaves the shining gold of faith to cool

And show what part is metal and what dross.
Hungering for fresh delights he throws around
Inquiring glances : lo ! the earth is bare !
Gone are his former pleasures, pastimes, rests,
The hopes and aspirations which sustained
Endeavor and the meager flesh-pots filled,
To quickened appetite in fancy sweet !
Gone are those friends whose service bought at least
A bone to beat back famine from the heart !
Earth is a boundless Wilderness, and life
A desert journey ! Then to murmuring,
Instead of prayer, he falls, whereat the skies,
Still merciful, rain angels' bread—the pure
Sweet distillations of celestial truth
And wisdom that, in gracious syllables,
Drop from God's Word and Spirit on the heart,
Bedewing all the morning walks of Thought.

Again day passes and the night comes down,
O'ershadowing mind and heart soon cold and dead
As a brown puff-ball which the traveler's foot
Presses, bringing forth only stifling fumes,
Like murmuring of unbelief, till Faith
Lays earnest hold upon the living Rock,
Whose streams burst forth amain, and all the soul
Water with the delights of pardoning love,
And make the desert blossom as the rose.

Soon before fire-crowned Sinai he stands,
Awestruck, while God, with sin-subduing voice,

Proclaims the Law of Righteousness, ordained
With tremblings and heart-burnings on the mount
Of Conscience, and with fiery finger traced
In the mind's plastic tablets. But alas!
Before the deed of his inheritance
Is signed, faith fails; the weak and groveling soul
Bows low before its Golden Calf—to works
Of human righteousness giving the praise
To the Invisible Glory due! Thereat
The skies grow lurid with the kindling flames
Of wrath! Destruction whets her sword; but Grace,
After sore chastisement and stern rebuke,
Renews the broken Covenant and builds
Therefor a Golden Ark, in whose defence,
The while God's statues, like a brazen yoke,
Are laid upon his heart to fetter sin,
The pilgrim journeys forward, feeding still
On manna from the bounteous skies. At length
He wearies of God's truth and yearns to taste
Once more of flesh and blood,—but sickens soon
Of words, words, words, infinite, endless words
That from the sea of mortal vanity
Come flocking like a deluge o'er his camp,
Making him glad once more to sit in peace,
Feeding on truths which through the morning's freshness
Rain silently from boughs of Paradise.

At last before his smiling Goal he stands,
The long-sought Land of Promise, from whose hills
Flow milk and honey, all the bosom sweets

And tender charities of life! but lo!
Instead of rest and freedom, frowning walls
Which graze the sky, and giant foes invite
His earnest toil and valor, at whose threats
The faithless soul melts like the morning dews
Before the summer sun. Murmuring he turns
From duty's thorny path, whereat the gates
Of Inward Peace and Liberty which stood
With outstretched arms to welcome his approach
With no dark river threatening death between,
Roll back and are so barred that neither wind
Of idle promises, nor rain of tears,
Nor courage, rising from despair too late,
Can break the firm decree, though, adding sin
To sin, presumptuous, rashly he essays,
Unaided, what, with God's defence, but late
He dared not, and soon learns not to despise
God's mandates, but most heartily his own
Untempered strength and wisdom. Back he flies,
Frantic with grief and shame, like one pursued
By bees, with anguish stung and keen remorse,
And makes his doleful penitentiary
Howl with his lamentations.
       Forty days
Of contradiction, chastisement and strife
He suffers there—as many years perhaps,
If these suffice not—wandering 'neath the rod
Of Moses, till the old, rebellious mind
Is slowly worn away, and the New Man
Again advances under leader new,—

No more by awe of Moses' rod constrained,
Or sense of duty urged to onerous tasks,
But by heart-strengthening Love and Hope inspired.
Strong in the Ark of Christ's redeeming might,
Up to death's forming rill, as to a bed
Of flowers, he hastes ; the nodding waves recede,
Wide spread the gales of Liberty, and Peace
And Joy bid hail to Canaan's blissful shore !

Thus from his school severe young Israel
Stepped nimbly to his native soil a man—
A nation among nations ! Now begins
The long and mid-day strife for eminence !
Unto no meaner seat has he been called
Than to the empire of the World :—" In thee
Shall all the nations of the Earth be blessed."
Go forward then conquering and to conquer !
Pluck all Earth's crowns and tread them 'neath thy feet,
Till every nation, kindred, tribe and tongue
Shall name itself The Israel of the Lord :—
This is thy task, achieve it ere night fall.

So forth he bounded, with a shout of faith
Mightier than the combined artillery
Of our twin hemispheres ! Down fell the walls
Of Jericho, Oppression's towering seat,
And onward marched the meek, exultant host,
Encountered brief repulse, from one fell seed
Of sin remaining, such as often mars
The noblest victory—the secret lust

Of gold and glory, by which men and states
Are drawn into the devil's net; but soon
The stern anathemas and burning wrath
Of an indignant People turn again
The withering glance of God upon his foes,
As each assailing throng, by madness urged
To their appointed doom, in turn receive
The meed of their iniquities, long due.

Then the sword rested from its toil, and sweet
But transitory Peace blessed Canaan's vales,
'Neath whose soft shining sun sin's lingering roots
Revived, as each new generation rose,
Causing the Husbandman again to drive
His yoke afield, and the rank sod o'erturn
With harsh affliction's plowshare. Every age
Its Winter had and Summer, Eve with Morn
Still alternating, as new races sprang,
And inwardly the selfsame path pursued
Which all their fathers trod—by sin enslaved,
By pitying Grace redeemed, as God to each
A mediate saviour and protector gave,—
Himself true Sovereign, on the Mercy Seat
Of Righteousness and Truth in light enthroned.

But when six times were past of Winter's cold
And Summer's growing heats, the restless Tribes
Once more conspired in general revolt,
As when their fathers built the Golden Calf.
"A king! a king!" to Samuel they cried:—

And kings they had, to their hearts' full content,
Who poisoned all the streams of liberty,
And turned them from their sighing Paradise
Into the great and terrible Wilderness
Of civil discord, anarchy and strife,
And Babylonish bondage—all that road
Which the mad Church with bloody footsteps trod,
And sackcloth garments, when she too would have
A king—whether Tradition, Pope, or Creed—
To bind men's free-born souls, on pain of death,
Or excommunication, to what man,
Daring to snatch the crown from Jesus' brow,
Declares to be the mandate of high Heaven.

Long, dark and bloody was the night which fell
On outcast Israel for that dread sin!
In it ten princedoms of the Chosen House
Perished, with Law and Temple now grown old,
And, like their builders, found incompetent
To lead God's People to enduring rest.

But morning dawned at last; a ruddy star,
Ascending from the Wilderness where sank
Judea's glory, kissed her eastern hills
And led her flocks to Jordan, whither came
The sacred Ark of a New Covenant,
With gold of faith o'erlaid and crowned with gold,
Whereon, in higher crown, the Mercy Seat
Of Love reposes, with the outstretched wings
Of Righteousness and Truth twin cherubim

That bear God's footsteps down to Earth, o'erspread.
Behind a veil of mystic imagery,
In a fair tabernacle from the gaze
Of sin-blind eyes concealed, her Saviour comes!
And, as the Sun of a New Era dips
His radiant feet in Jordan, the dark veil
Which shrouds the inner Temple of the Skies,
Hiding from man his heavenly home, divides
A moment to the eye of Faith, and Peace
Descending crowns the Son of God and Man!

Rise, captive daughter of Jerusalem,
And kiss the Son, the High and Virgin-born,
And take the empire of a waiting World!
What! dost thou not behold Him? Lo, He stands
Beside thee, meek and spotless as the lamb
Which Abel chose for a peace-offering
To Heaven, well pleased! more intimate with God
In contemplative walk and ministry
Than Enoch, or him chosen second sire
Of human kind! than Abraham more firm
In faith! a sweeter sacrifice for sin
Than Isaac! more than Jacob resolute
To win God's blessing! more magnanimous
Than Joseph! mightier to break the yoke
Of sin, and lead God's People to repose,
Than the great Lawgiver, or him named
The saviour, valiant Joshua! in strength
Excelling him who rent the lion's jaws!
Judge more immaculate than Samuel!

Of kinglier heart and more melodious lips
Than Judah's royal bard ! than Solomon
With more imperial wisdom crowned ! in zeal
Exceeding the great Tishbite and his son—
The Law's defender and man's succorer !
Of prophets chief, though rapt Isaiah lift
God's trumpet to his lips and pour vast waves
Of transcendental music from Heaven-gate
Down through the echoing ages ! more beloved
Than Daniel, and the last of evening's train
Excelling, as the Sun that star excels
Whose golden fingers lift the latch of dawn !
Lo, where he stretches out his godlike arm
And hurls the powers of darkness from their seat
In body, soul and spirit ! None can stand
Before him ! From his magic finger flies
Disease, with limping sore Infirmity !
Devils and Death slink from his burning glance,
Like Night and Winter from the rising Sun !
O'er all the desolate and moaning Land,
Wrapped in the icy winding-sheet of sin
And ignorance, descend the mellowing floods
Of life and light, till, like a mountain stream
Leaping o'er crags, or storm-tossed Galilee,
The people wave, and clap their hands, and shout
"Hosanna unto David's Son, our King !"

Alas ! what hast thou done ? Whose form is that
Suspended on yon dripping cross ? Oh ! Oh !
It is thy Lord ! thy Life ! thy Light ! thy Crown !

Thy Peace! thy Joy! thy Immortality!
All, all are gone! all dead! all crucified!
O wretched mother of a murderous throng!
Get thee unto the wilderness! The Grave
Awaits thy coming! Outcast, desolate,
Earth has no home for thee in her breadth!
Afar, the eagles scent the feast of blood!
Near, lights funereal to the desert lead!

But hark! there is a murmur in the air
Of singing voices! hark! there is in earth
A rustling! Say, were not these bones all dry?
Were not these ashes dead? What meaneth then
This army rising as in mockery
Of Death and Hell—clothing their giant frames
With living flesh—sinews and blood and skin—
And catching from the winds of heaven their breath?
Lo! they go forth in twelve invincible bands
That toss a smile at Death and through the grave
Rush on to victory, increasing more
The more their blood is spilt! From every drop
Spring up ten warriors with Truth's lightning armed,
With shields of adamant and swords of keen
Celestial temper!—On! and on! and on!
Till Rome's proud empire trembles in their grasp,
Till distant lands, with tongues of strange accent,
Barbaric tribes and lettered capitols,
All bend the knee, and unto Israel's King
Confess allegiance, and join their might
To roll his conquering chariot round the World!

There came a stranger to my rude abode.
   And unto me, with flattering accent, said,
" I know a pathway leading from this wood
Along a toilsome but delightful road
   To yonder mountain's gold-enameled head."

Straightway I followed him, eager to gain
   The lofty seat. Up many a flowering height
He led me till thoughts of the shadowy plain
Despised:—far over it the sun-kissed main
   Glimmered, and all my heart with joy was light.

The path grew rugged, but I heeded not:
   It grew precipitous, but still I rose:
My brain grew dizzy and my blood was hot;
But just above appeared a level spot,
   Which having gained, I there would take repose.

I reached it and my lids began to drop,
   And my lax nerves to suck at Nature's breast:
Then said my guide, " If you would win the top
You must not lean upon the idler's prop,
   But make the paths of industry your rest."

So, I aroused my blood-shot eyes and brain
   To further toil, and spurred them to the strife
With a right-earnest will: the twinge of pain
I counted but the needful prize of gain;—
   To him who wins the mark, oh, what is life!

Weary, I sought a more circuitous lead
   The next bold steep to scale: but, as I strove
To mount a jutting crag, it seemed indeed
As if that mountain trembled like a reed
   And shook me back into my native grove.

And then I woke and saw that I had dreamed
   A strange, wild, earnest dream of human life:
And, as I deeply mused thereon, it seemed
As if an angel through the twilight gleamed,
   And beckoned me unto a nobler strife.

II.

FROM long discursion, as a traveler
   Standing upon the Alps far forth surveys
The country he would visit, not on wings
Of raptured vision borne, but stepping down
With difficulty to the common road
Of dusty toil and strife, my humble tale
I now resume, intending to relate
What happened in the inmost life of one
Six years my junior, sister, pupil, friend
And partner of those inmost thoughts which shrink
From gaze of others well beloved—twin soul,
More feminine, more delicately wise
And weak and fair, from infancy the joy
And comfort of our house, till Sorrow laid
His cross upon her brow—our Morning Star,
Our last born on the Earth and first in Heaven.

We thresh the sheaf and cast away the straw
And winnow out the chaff; we grind the grain,
And bolt the flour; then take the finest part,
And mixing it with sugar, milk and eggs,
And spices brought from India or the South,

Make a dessert to set before our friends;
They eat, or taste, after their solid meal,
And go their way expecting something new
To-morrow. Thus the poet builds his song,
Taking from life's best growths the delicate pith,
Enriching it with cream from his own soul,
And sugar from the presses of his heart,
And quick conceits out of his fertile brain,
Spicing with native or with borrowed wit,
He mingles them with patient industry,
Refines them in his intellectual fires
And sets them on your table. Daintily
You touch or eat, and at to-morrow's feast
Expect some new dessert of song—which he
Who would provide, fit for the growing thought
Of an immortal soul,—not destitute
Of wholesome nourishment while with the warmth
Of pure afflatus filled,—must go again
Into the crucible, and there invoke
The Sire of song to send his only Son,
Immortal Truth, Imagination's lord,
With him to walk amid the fervid flames
Of heart and soul and intellect aglow
With sevenfold heats of passion,—there to keep
The even poise of judgment, cool as when
The North Wind sports with Eve, and bring him forth
Without the smell of anguish in his robes.
Thus I entreat as I essay to glean
Out of the many things which love holds dear,
However common, what may please the taste

Of those whose minds are full of pleasant things—
Vast galleries of Art stored with all wealth
Of genius, noblest out of noble culled,
That can no mean companionship endure.
Yet not alone to please do I aspire,
But through the gate called Beautiful to lead
The wisdom-loving soul, or the tried heart
Whose fondling on Faith's altar must be laid,
Into the sacred Temple where God keeps
The substance of those shadows which do seem
To form our human life.
                              It was my lot,
Chosen by partial confidence, to give
Companionship and counsel to this fair
And zealous Pilgrim, when by Heavenly Grace
Invited to exchange the fading hopes
Of earth for garments of celestial dye,
And take her journey to the Promised Land,
There to attend the court of Him whose name
She long had honored, and his counsel held
In chief respect. Now, more than honor due
To Teacher wise, or Sovereign, He desired
The conjugal devotion of a spirit
Inflamed with love's heart-welding fires, and bound,
For life and death, for woe and weal to One
Than life or liberty more dear. So called,
She looked upon her garments and perceived
They were not meet to clothe a Prince's bride.
Of coarse and sullen texture they appeared,
Stained here and there with various ugly blots

Of sin and patches of discordant hue.
Yet had she not another: so her heart
Grew sad and melancholy even to tears,
That she must be seen at the King's palace,
If seen at all, so wretchedly attired.
Meanwhile the messenger made haste, for time
Was pressing, and the King's command he said,
Was urgent, that no needless vanity
Should interfere with love, but filial trust
And confidence atone for past neglect
By prompt obedience to present duty.

So through the channel of the sea he led her,
From which emerging, after no small strife
With sorrow and dismay, her garments shone
More brightly in the rising Sun of hope
And love, soft smiling now over the waves,
Where slumbered all the World's alluring shows—
Its pride, its power, its fame, its glory, dust.

Advancing toward the Wilderness, the light
Of faith grew sometimes dim, and hunger preyed
Upon the heart, cut off from Nature's springs
Of pleasure, and incompetent to bear
The unrestrained effulgence of the Skies.
But, of an affable and patient spirit,
Not many murmurs rose of discontent,
Before the heavenly showers began to fall
About our pathway. Joyful then it was
To see her feed upon that mystic bread,

From everything in Nature gathering
Instruction and delight. Flower, leaf and stone,
Even the desert sands, were radiant
With a poetic glow of imagery
Peculiar to Love's charmèd spring ; the clouds
Dropped knowledge, and each wind with honey-dew,
Odors and balm, came laden. From the Rock
Abundant waters flowed ; the mountains blazed,
And spoke in thunder tones, proclaiming Love
To God and man, life's everlasting Law ;
Fair was the Tabernacle of the Lord,
Adorned with gold, with azure curtains veiled !
Fairest the Ark of His Redeeming Love !
The cloud of His protecting providence
Was almost to the eye of sense revealed ;
His Spirit, a safe counsellor and guide,
Made plain the path of duty in the midst
Of thick-strewn doubts and perils.

       Thus through all
The varying phases of that wondrous journey
Which men and Nations must alike pursue,
When to the higher life of Freedom called,
Our Traveler passed in safety, till arrived
Upon the borders of the Promised Land,
Where, as a youth schooled in the mysteries
Of Art and Science takes his blade or pen,
His plow or pruning hook, to join life's battle,
Or toils of manly industry, the soul,
Instructed in the laws and mysteries,
Of the celestial life, yearns to engage

In virtue's sacred warfare, or in arts
Diviner of domestic love and peace.
Thus, by the Spirit urged to leave the walks
Of solitude and join Immanuel's host,
Battling, with broken ranks, to rid the world
Of Sin's prolific broods, her maiden heart,
Modest and reticent, in evil hour
Gave heed to its false spies, to Fear and Doubt
Lending the ear, rather than Faith and Hope,
God's witnesses. Turning from duty's call,
She would have fled, but worse calamity
Saw in retreat, with loss insufferable
Threatened, of all her heart esteemed most dear.
Thus thrown into confusion, sore distressed
By her unfaithfulness, she sought again
To advance, and craved new opportunities
To prove her love sincere. Nor was her prayer
Denied, but vainly granted ; all her powers
In thraldom lay to some mysterious spell :
A willing spirit had no will to move
Rebellious flesh to action till the hour
Of new probation passed. Then Conscience poured
Her blows like rain and all the face of Heaven
Grew black with gathering storms, at sight of which,
Instead of flying to the only refuge
For sinners built of God, Love's Golden Ark,
With unbought grace and saving knowledge stored,
She only begged of Him another chance
To save herself.
    Oh! it was agony

But to look on that conflict, as she strove,
With a persistence which had once o'erborne
The power of generous Nature, to atone
For her ingratitude by some good act
Of pure obedience that should unlock
The gates of her lost Paradise!

       Too long
Mute witness of the wasting strife I stood,
Trusting that He who had so well begun
Would finish his good work without aid asked
Of mortal tongue, but soon my error learned,
When, as I mused amid my garden toils,
She came and said to me with bated breath
As one breaks news of woe, "'Tis over now;
I have received my sentence, and have come
To say a sad and long farewell to you:'
And with a clinging accent on the 'you'
She clutched my heart as with the iron grasp
Of one in drowning agonies.

       O Christ!
In that dread hour I saw, and wondered not,
How thou couldst leave the throne of bliss, and fly
Beneath Death's lifted dart and pour thy blood
Like water on its breast to bring back hope
Into the fading eye of a lost World!
Taking thereof, unto these pallid lips
I pressed the soul-reviving anodyne,
Pleading a Saviour's love, stronger than death,
Stronger than that to which death seemed a joy,
The double death when drear Gethsemane

Echoed his moans, and the relenting Cross
Shook with that cry which veiled the pitying Sun,
" Eloi ! Eloi ! lama sabbacthani ? "
For thee, sad soul, that cry went up to Heaven
And brought down rest—rest for the bleeding heart
Which in its uttermost extremity
Still adds to every plea, " Thy will be done."

" Alas, my brother, with the balm still comes
A thorn for troubled conscience ! Is it well
To say Thy will be done, and lift no hand
To do what God requires ?—so unlike Him
Who bore his cross till on it he was borne ? "

" Yet even He, in his humanity,
Was found too weak to bear his cross alone ;
He staggered 'neath his burden and at last
Gave up, in utter nothingness of self,
To bear God's just rebuke against a World
Which having sinned, can no more keep His law,
Unhelped of grace, than death can bring forth life."

" But grace will help when we a helping hand
Obediently put forth, powerless till then
For our deliverance. It is for this
My Saviour long has waited, long has plead
With my rebellious will to bear the yoke
Of God's commands, beneficent and light,
But for my heart's amazing wickedness."

"Say rather its infirmities : 'The spirit
Indeed is willing but the flesh is weak.'
Ev'n in the face of mortal agonies
The earth-bound soul will slumber till the voice
Of its rejected Lord, whose least command
It cannot keep till tears of blood have flowed
From his fond bosom, wakens it again
To consciousness and shame ; and even then
It can but fly his side in the dark hour
Of peril when the secret sin which walks
In company with honest purposes—
When glory-loving Selfishness, betrays
The Son of God to death. But He resigns
Only his mortal part, from man assumed,
That he might rescue it from Sin's embrace,
And death, inseparable shade of sin.
Returning presently He will uplift
Both his and our united manhood, purged
Of those impurities which so long clog
The spirit's action, making it the slave
Of Weakness and Disease, Sin's fertile race.

" This is the glorious work He now had wrought
In my frail body, clothing it with strength
To bear the spirit's weight, had I obeyed
His quickening commands. From first to last
Man has a part to do in life's great work,
Else no more life, but idle mimicry,
A barren pantomime of Nature's powers.
If to the soul no righteous act belong,

Whence the distinction between faith and sin?
What more is man than a wind-shaken harp,
Or sea-voiced organ with ten thousand keys,
On which when God has played some heavenly airs
With his right hand, He sweeps it with his left,
And makes it groan harsh discords, just to prove
The first was music and expose the effect?
Wherefore methinks 'tis time this truant vine,
So tenderly nourished, cease to cast its fruit.

"Ah, who shall say, 'tis time? Tis ever time
That Sin had not o'erwhelmed the world in death;
That Earth had wakened from her dreams and stood,
In marriage robes of light and love arrayed,
To meet her Lover hastening from the Skies.
Time draws the kink in many an argument,
And only he can disentangle it.
But Time is sick and seldom keeps his hour,
And halt and blind withal, for when Sin pierced
His eye with her foul dart, he backward ran
A thousand leagues into the wilderness
Of ancient Night, dragging his shattered coach,
With its wrenched axil and crazed bridal pair,
In ruins after him. Christ reined him back;
But only He who holds the rein now knows
His place: man ever sets his post too near,
Because it shines with such a goodly light,
That, like the sun, it seems but a bare league
From every generation:—nor indeed
Is it from their world farther; so 'tis well:—

But the great World has a much larger day,
And the great Man who draws his life from it,
As doth an unhatched eaglet from the egg,
Is but a weak and puling infant yet,
In virtue, though his head be like Mont Blanc
In vanity and sin. Thereat both Truth
And Mercy may with Equity rejoice,
In hope that slow bespeaks a solid growth.
Hark you, should he whose dust Heaven did refine
Six generations of the stars—his soul
As long revolved in God's creative thought—
Who, poised at last upon Creation's spire,
To face God's breath and glitter back his smile,
Did let the devil throw him to the ground
And ne'er cry Hold—not holding fast the rod
Of God's command like Him who, later, stood
On Salem's Temple to reclaim his right
By simple faith—shall this poor shifting vane,
Broken, defiled and battered by its fall,
Mount back again o'er the enormous pile
Of lightning-blasted Nature in an hour?
Or when by matchless goodness from the mire
Drawn forth, and washed in Mercy's crimson streams,
Shall it of its own power and virtue boast?
Or dream of glory? Not a single stair
Shall he be lugged, but he shall give God thanks,
Even that he could consent to be thus drawn
Out of the rubbish of his fallen house.
How can the dead arise? Can he put forth
A motion of his will, or animate

Desire, whence motion springs, till in him God
Replant uprooted power and liberty?
Power planted is God's talent, freely lent,
For beggared man to merchant with and gain
A livelihood or competence, in trust
Of his kind Benefactor who, betimes,
Calls for both interest and principal,
His due, that we may not forget our thanks,
And, freely rendering up our borrowed wealth,
A double portion from His hand receive.

"Or the just doom which for the idler waits—
To be outcast from His indignant presence
To utter darkness. But, because most just,
I cannot bear my punishment, like Cain
A vagabond henceforward in the Earth,
Till to her sighing breast she kindly takes
The blood-stained clod, haply with penal flames
To purify it for some better use—
The thing that stained it gone to other fires,
As fearfully beneficent and just.
Have I not crucified the Son of God
Afresh, and put his love to open shame
Before the angels? O ungrateful soul!
Whom hast thou but thy rank iniquities
To blame for fruitless penance self-incurred?

" Nay, thou hast but, through impotence of faith,
Sin-born, yet by redeeming love atoned,
Declined his offered service, like the twelve

Who fled his presence at the fiery hour
Of trial, but withdrew not thence their hearts,
Fast bound to his in agonizing love.
Till love of Goodness for its own sweet sake,
And pure desire of virtue's crown, be dead,
Sin may destroy the outgrowth of the life
Invisible, but touches not its root,
Which, watered by the crimson rain of Heaven,
A thousand times will spring with hope, and lift
Its pleading palms in air, nor once receive
From the glad, pitying Sun a cold rebuke."

"But are not all moving toward Heaven or Hell
By slow gradations? Distant seems the goal,
And easy of escape, where Folly leads
The pleasure-loving throng down the broad road
Of self-indulgence—distant never less,
Through Fancy's glass beheld ; but every step
A step more near, diminishes at once
The power and wish to change, while the poor soul
Grows ever more absorbed, more bound with cords
Of habit, till at last, though with some warmth
Of nature moved, or lingering sparks of grace,
It grows oblivious to God's kind voice,
Fainter and fainter through the twilight heard
Calling it back to life, and, step by step,
Like an old man descending to the grave,
Sinks down into the shades of endless night.
Oh! from this horrible doom it is I flee,
Till my weak limbs can bear me on no more,
And my poor brain grows dizzy with its flight."

"Then let us no more strive, but prostrate fall,
Here at the foot of this red, weeping cross,
Which only bars that melancholy road.
O Father of the fatherless, and Friend
Of the oppressed! Helper omnipotent
Of them that have no strength, the grievous load
Of our infirmities and wickedness
Take from us, for the love of thy dear Son,
Whose blood our sins have shed, and on us pour
That renovating stream, that our cold hearts,
All empty, dead, corrupt without thy grace,
May henceforth beat in unison with thine,
And more reflect thy goodness, truth and love."

"Amen, and yet amen ; so shall we do
God's mandates and no more despise his law,
Most meet to be obeyed. O had I stood
Faithful in trial's hour, his mighty arm
Had girded me to run the glorious race
Of immortality, as when of old
Elijah ran before the king! My voice
Like an apostle had rung forth to call
Mankind to peace and freedom! All the Earth
Had listened and believed, all nations joined
Immanuel's conquering host, beating their swords
To plowshares and their spears to pruning-hooks,
Never to learn war more,—in nobler arts
And heavenly industries employed. But see!
He comes again! my dear Redeemer comes
With offers new of mercy! I will now

Be still and let Him lift me to his arms,
And kiss away my tears, and pour sweet balm
Into my crying wounds, and lift my feet
Over this narrow stream to Canaan's banks,
All beautiful with virtue's fadeless blooms!—
Lo, He has passed! the vision fades! the cloud
Returns and closes darkly round my soul,
No more to lift its awful gloom!"
        —Alas,
There is no death but death; no royal road
From Earth to Heaven but that the King has trod:
And no man ere, like Him, gave up the ghost
By his own motion; whether this or that
We will, the act is life. Smite then O God!
And slay in thy own fashion—one with fire,
And one with frost, with lightning one, and one
With lingering plagues!—ten thousand ministers
Wait thy command to purge our souls of pride,
And scour our vessels of mortality:
But this seems hardest—this the bitterest cup
For mortals mixed—to be thrust back from Heaven
Into a living grave, where soul and mind
Disjointed fall apart, as bone from bone
And flesh from flesh—there 'mid delusive hopes
And mocking phantoms of delight, to feel
The gnawing worm rankle amid the nerves
Of consciousness, and the insatiate fire
Pluck at life's elements, till all is still
As dust in the cold coffin. From this hell
Great God deliver us! Did He lie there,

Who drank each cup offered to human lips,
And wrung the dregs? Aye, at the midnight hour,
When all his bosom friends—bone of his bone,
Flesh of his flesh—fell from him, and when Thou,
Soul of his soul, stood from his soul aloof,
An awful moment—when the iron Earth
And brazen Sky no pitying tear let fall,
But the World's broken bond left him to pay
To the last farthing, that a bankrupt race
Might from his soul's exhaustless treasures draw
Perpetual ransom—then his spirit felt
Death's terrors; then his judgment was removed,
His light became as darkness, and his strength
Ashes:—the grave was then a place of rest.
But lo! that gulf which like the Dead Sea drank
Jordan's perpetual tribute, and still cried
"Give! give! I thirst!" and, deep beneath the main,
Rolled on its leaden billows, soon o'erflowed,
When Heaven's vast Ocean rose and poured its floods
Into her seething cauldron. Hell's huge maw,
Which gorged a race and still grew cavernous,
As when Leviathan sucks at a draught
A billion insects dancing on the waves
Over the unseen jaws of Destiny,
Soon felt strange surfeit when that Meteor fell
On Time's dark waters and sank glistening down
Into its rock-ribbed, wondering vault. Alarmed,
The Grave spouts forth her Conqueror, and Death
Amazed, retreats and falls on his own sword.
O Father! let it then suffice that we

Approach our foes but near enough to mark
What our Deliverer has done,—as when
One looks upon a lion slain, and feels
His iron muscles, and inserts his hand
Between those jaws horrent in death, to learn
How to give thanks to Jesse's warlike son,
Who stripped his fierceness off, yea, in one hour
Made both the lion and the bear as tame
As the meek lambs which else had rinsed their fangs.

"Brother I fain would sleep : my soul is sad
And weary unto death with this long strife.
Yet dare I not my lids in slumber close,
Lest they no more should open on a world
Of beauty, sweet to sight and ravished hope,
Though justly to unworthy feet denied."

"O heart to mine most dear ! how would I fain
Take from my life its joys and make them thine,—
Its rest to give thy soul an hour's repose !
But One far worthier has already claimed
That noble privilege. O think of Him
Who had not where to lay his star-crowned head—
Star-crowned in Heaven but girt with thorns on Earth ;
For us He bore the weariness and want,
The sorrows, disappointments, buffetings,
Pains and asperities of human life,
Slights from the erring good, and contumely
From wicked men, that to the desolate
And broken heart He might apply the balm

Of his all-healing sympathy and love.
This heavenly cordial take, darling, and rest;
For so He giveth his beloved sleep."

"What! shall my heart rejoice while He lies there
Pale, silent, motionless in the cold grave,
Where my ingratitude has laid Him? No:
Let sorrow rather be its joy, and tears
Its pleasant wine, till my obedience
Permits Him to arise and take the crown
Of Righteousness and place it on my brow—
Crown ever his, by mercy magnified
In glory, but in triumph only worn
When with his ransomed, loving children shared.
Say, doth a father more in clemency
Delight than commendation of his child?
Obedience reflects the highest praise,
And none like Mercy grieves to have been born,
And longs to fly again to her warm nest,
And sleep forever in Love's blissful heart."

"Most true and honorable are these words,
Dear casuist, yet not the whole of truth.
For Israel's penitence, or deeds of faith
And virtue by his frail disciples shown,
Jesus had vainly waited in the tomb.
But rising thence through God's eternal power,
He lifted his dead Body, his fair Spouse,
O'erwhelmed with condemnation, from the grave
Of buried hope, and poured the healing oil

Of his undying love upon her wounds,
And gave her strength, after a brief repose,
To do and dare and suffer for his name.
Then, turning from her idle dreams of power
And glory, dead to every thought of self,
She followed her ascending Lord from Earth
To love's celestial Paradise ; or rather
That Paradise came down to Earth, when He,
With all his holy angels, through the clouds
Of human expectation and desire,
Broke like the sun through noon-day storms, and poured
The tender radiance of benignant love
And self-denying goodness on her breast.
So let us patiently His rising wait."

Huntsman when the chase is done,
If the game be lost or won,
 Unstring thy Bow:
Farther toward the morning sun
 Shall be its throw.

Youth whose soft arms haste to toil,
Or whose brain to learning's spoil,
 Unstring thy Bow,
Ere excess consume like oil
 Thy spirit's flow.

Miner in the mines of thought,
Seeking where no man hath sought,

Regard thy Bow!
Oft the crown is worn that's wrought
 The sod below.

Diver in the soul's deep sea,
Pearls of peace and liberty
 If thou wouldst know,
Take what Jesus bringeth thee,
 And rest thy Bow.

III.

REST! can the parched, vein-shrunken traveler rest
    In sight of the blue heaven of liquid life,—
Whether oasis or mirage,—that charms
His captive eye and nerves his weary limbs?
On! on! and Mercy grant it be no dream!
What though my trusty camel fails at last
And kneels upon the sand?—I must more speed
To drink and bring him back a needful bowl,
To prove that God is to his promise true,
And when He calls means we shall follow Him.

Great God! she reels! she staggers! help her Thou!
My staff is broken; I am but a worm
Writhing with anguish in the burning sun—
The fierce, red glare of this impending woe!
O why wilt Thou give strength neither to rest,
Nor labor?—light to see, nor dark to sleep?
But only this distracting hornèd moon
Of an unfinished Law, big with the child
Of Gospel Hope, which many times goes down
Before it is fulfilled and turns to wane?
Have pity and reveal Thy quickening Beam
Unto the void eye of her struggling soul,

Before too late. One ray from Thy bright throne
Is worth a thousand tapers lit by men:
One little breath of Thine can swell the sail
Which thrice a thousand human arguments
Puff at in vain. O why should this fair bud
Wither on its dry stalk, while in my branch
Flows life which would but cannot that way bleed
To save a dying sister? Why should this
Of all Thy radiant blushes fail for thirst,
While tantalizing waves laugh round her lips,
And golden apples nod to her very teeth?
Must the last spark of heavenly fire go out,
And leave our souls but black, unsightly stuff,
Ere we confess all glory Thine? O breathe,
Breathe on the fading coal, and quicken it
Once more to joyous, heaven-aspiring flame!
Strong men go up, knock, enter and find rest,
Leaving their sin-soiled, blood-stained rags without:
But now a tender maiden seeks Thy door
Almost in marriage robes attired, when, lo!
Thou bid'st her come, and in Thy bosom hidest
Thy death-dispelling hand, and from her eye
Thy latch-revealing beam, till her sick brain
Reels like a drunken mast with tattered sails
Flapping the angry wind—yea till the god
Within her, trembles on his blazing throne,
And all the steadfast planetary powers
Threaten to fly their orbits! Father in Heaven,
The night is dark, the storm is very sore,
Open Thy bosom to Thy houseless ones!

Dear slumbering Helmsman, wake! carest Thou not
Though we all perish? Speak unto these winds,
And they shall slink into their caves abashed,
While from Thy lips flow tranquilizing oil,
To make the tossed soul mirror Thy calm trust.

Then, to the mountain tops of faith upraised,
Prophetic vision blessed my wondering eyes.
I saw the scattered fragments of that rare,
Heaven-favored nation who, for conscience sake
Hugging her golden fetters, cast her crown
Of glory in the dust, which there to find,
God sent her, with consuming stroke and flame
On her fair idols, overwhelming all
Her cherished hopes with ruin infinite
And helpless anguish. Lo! as one deranged,
Pursuing shadows, from her blissful seat
Exiled, she wanders in all lands! Confused,
Blasted and torn, a nation without head,
Her fame inverted, lost her high renown,
She roams the world's vast wilderness transformed
From bare to bloom by the rejected grace
Poured from the bosom of her smitten Rock!
Disconsolate she treads the spire-crowned streets
Of New Jerusalem, seeking the shade
Of her departed glory, long since cast
Amid time's rubbish, like a broken loom
On which the royal garments once were woven,
Or nest from which the eaglets have escaped,
By whirlwinds on the barren mountain strewn.

But though, as rolls Love's purple chariot
Through Zion's broadening avenues and lanes,
That tearless maiden, with dishevelled crown,
Sighing amid the tombs of buried hopes,
Be passed as one unnoticed, while most seen
By Abraham's God and David's Lord, still dear
For memory's sake, and the immutable bond
Of solemn promise, and poetic truth
Of conjugal affection once bestowed,
Nearest the Father's and the Lover's heart
She stands, chosen of Mercy to receive
The key of Earth's great day, and place the crown
Of love's supreme achievement on the brow
Her blindness pierced with thorns: to clothe again
Those limbs in purple, dyed in her own heart;
To kiss the feet and hands through which she drove
The cruel nails, and staunch that bleeding side
With her soft bosom! To this end she waits,
Neglected yet a little while, the hour
When, from the circle of his conquering march
Through the great Gentile body of mankind,
Neglected for her sake that Life might spring
From her engrafted fountain, and in turn
Ransomed through her despoiling, Jesus comes,
With proof invincible, his titles high
To claim—Sovereign Redeemer of the World,
The Lord of Sabbaoth and Salem's King.

Then with the prophet "O the depth!" I cried,
"The riches of His wisdom who hath joined

So well this fair mysterious frame of being,
That while one member dips in Jordan's waves,
Another standing firmly on the shore,
Or half immersed, extends a helping hand
To guide it through the depths, then bowing low
In turn the sanctifying rite receives.
Thus Soul and Body, Jew and Gentile thus,
By Heaven's benignant ordinance are joined."

But what shall turn Euphrates from her course,
Or win this limnèd spirit from its dark
Entanglements? Caught in the narrow strait
'Twixt duty and sin-born incompetence,
With loss of coveted delights, and storm
Of anguish threatened, the bewildered soul,—
Turning no more at Reason's call to view
The substance of its hopes, and truer truths
Learn from experience,—with steadfast gaze
Burns after the impossible—the fair
Receding Vision of Life's Summer-land,
Radiant with love's imperishable bloom,
And wisdom's golden fruit.   What horror then,
What blankness of amazement on our hearts
Fell like the shadow of an unforetold
Eclipse, throwing its weird and awful gloom
O'er palsied industry and joy, when Doubt
Could no more doubt the melancholy tale,
By the wild flickerings of fancy told,
That Reason had received a shock.   Too long

And desperately bent on the bright dream
Of glory just beyond her straining grasp,
The mental eye grew fixed, and the vexed nerve,
Weary with its unbroken tension, burned
With fever heat, and its own morbid flames
Mingled with the communicated light
Of nature and of grace, till, in the maze
Of thought's commingling elements, the true
And false danced hand in hand, pleasure gave birth
To pain, and Grief rejoiced that she could grieve.
Thus out of order chaos came again ;
Darkness from light, and evil from the seeds
Of promised good sprang up. Satan was lord,
And on His cross the Sun of Righteousness
Bowed down His thorn-crowned head and slept, while Death
Triumphing stood and raised his glittering dart,
Wrapped round with flowers of a delusive hope,
As the insidious fowler thus prepared
His last and fatal snare. "One effort more,"
He whispered "and this tedious conflict ends ;
In victory ends. What doth thy Lord desire ?—
What ask, but certain proof that nought in Earth
Attracts thee like His love ? Then let thy heart
No more defile itself with carnal joys,
Nor taste the world's gross condiments till bread
Be given it from Heaven, with love's pure wine,
Fresh from its fountain in the Heart of Bliss.
No more let human love or counsel turn
Thy spirit from its purpose, drawing back

'Thy feet from Jordan's puny stream, which soon
Will fly before life's conquering Ark, when once
Thy faithfulness is proved. At the last hour,
Jesus, well-pleased, will from His cloudy throne
Descend, and lift thee from the smiling floods
Of thy transmuted sorrow, to a seat
At his right hand, eternal, glorious,
And crown thee with acceptance, honor, love,
In sight of thy rejoicing friends, more blessed,
By thy devoted constancy and faith,
Than by a weak surrender to their fears."
So spake the arch-deceiver, by whose power,
When the true miracle of life is past,
And God to His pavilion has returned,
A mocking semblance of the truth is built
Of life's abandoned forms, whereby the heart,
Half won to liberty, but thirsting still
For gain and glory more than godliness,
And leaning on the arm of human strength,
Is backward lured to the devouring pit,
Where all things mortal are consumed :—so spake,
And to his subtleties her ear gave heed,
As to an angel's voice.
     O darkest hour
Of mortal darkness! when, with iron will,
Clenched by a drowning conscience, she refused
All food and consolation till the Sun
Of her lost hope should rise! Make haste! no more
Of sign and shadow! Stern realities
Of famine, torch and sword are at thy gates,

Devoted, frantic, blind Jerusalem!
A serpent's glistening coil is round thee twined,
Too strong for mortal arm! O Death! how sweet
Thy pure and orderly comings are, when Love,
Home-bound, flings back her fond farewell, and glides
Out of the weary, pallid, restful form,
To seek the mansions of eternal joy,
Or hover, in sweet memories, round the hearth
And table with their vacant seat, not all
Vacant, and round the evening lamp which shines
With a more spiritual radiance on the page
By the present absent-ones most loved! But Oh!
Glare not upon us from the vacant eyes
Of those we have adored—those whom we love
More than the best blood of our curdling hearts,
Which longs for their deliverance to leap forth
And plead with the destroyer!
      Vain, all vain,
Is a fond father's mandate, little used
To such respect;—as vain a mother's tears,
More powerful still. A sister's tender plea,
A brother's calm appeal alike are vain.
No: to a higher mandate, and a love
Profounder, she will this time faithful prove—
Faithful to death a crown of life to gain.
So clung bewildered Mary to the cross
Where hung her dying Lord, expecting soon
To see the Conqueror of Death and Hell
Transform that wretched scaffold to the throne
Of an adoring world. What wonder, when

The light divine faded from those fond eyes
Which had been her chief solace, and which oft
She had in vision seen, regal with joy
Beneath the crown of Solomon, she fain
Had perished also on the crimson sod
Where o'erwrought reason swooned?
                              Three dreadful days
At the grave's mouth she lay as one entranced,
Bound by some strange, mysterious power, as when
A dove before the serpent's ghastly jaws
Stands motionless, ready, another moment,
To stuff his burning throat. Then, summoning
Counsel both human and divine, I sought
Once more her couch, and twining tenderly
The cords of reason round her dormant soul,
Seized gently, but with strong, inflexible grasp
Of will her sturdy purpose, adding "must"
To vain persuasions. Thus aroused, the fiend
In her distempered brain flashed fire and hurled
Defiance; but I saw that he was chained
By the strong angel who kept guard of him
In Love's invincible name. Then adding strength
To inward power, I raised her drooping form
Half upright, and there held, while from my eyes
She drank the calm, fixed purpose. Swift along
The tremulous nerves the clear conviction flashed
That time was ripe for change—that Truth had spoken
The edict of a stern necessity,
To draw her from the grave of a dead hope
Back to life's cold realities.   Alas!

How could she bear Earth's mockeries again?
That silent tomb, with its pale, princely Guest,
Was sweeter than a Christless world :—and then
She sank again upon her couch and clung,
In tearless agony, to her fond dream,
But with a hold less resolute, less firm.
Slowly she bent her conquered will to mine,
First struggled hard, then half embraced the chain,
Revolted, yielded, threatened, scolded, plead;
But still from self-imprisonment came forth,
Looked on the face of Nature, and partook,
Reluctantly, her bounty, looked on life,
As from a frozen mountain-top, erewhile
With glory crowned, a stranded aëronaut,
His heaven-bound bark to sudden anchor drawn,
Gazes abroad over a mist-clad world,
In servile toils or sensuous pleasures lost.
On Home, the scene of conflicts and defeats
Immeasurably sad, she dared not look,
But with averted thoughts walked to and fro
Amid its faded blooms, striving to shun
The stings with which e'en love itself seemed armed,
To drive her from its doors.
                         So she went forth,
An exile from her native paradise,
Just forty days, as by her chronicles
Long afterwards I read. Her silken chain
Freely transferring to the faithful hand
Of a devoted sister wise to mark
The delicate needs of health, she went abroad

A wanderer in the World's vast wilderness,
Obedient to the law of others' wills,
And the imperative demands of health,
That the exhausted nerve, relaxing soon
To infant tenderness, might drink new life,
Rest and diversion, from the mingled springs
Of nature, social intercourse and art.
Soon heart and brain regained their equipoise;
Love in her eyes and laughter on her lips
Resumed their favorite seat. Returning then,
Lovely as Dian after brief eclipse,
But with an inward sadness, half concealed
In kindness from her friends, and with a doubt
If she at all were thought of in the Skies,
She gave such diligence as feeble health
Permitted, to alleviate the ills
Of poor humanity, finding in these,
Not the gilt crucifix which anchorites
In caves and dim cathedrals bow before,
Nor that, as vain, in duties self-imposed,
But the true cross which the meek Lamb of God
For our deliverance and example bore,
Formed of the rude, harsh growths of common life—
The manifold afflictions and restraints,
Humiliations, hungerings, conflicts, deaths,
To which the child at once of Earth and Heaven
Must needs be subject in a sin-wrecked World.

Yet He not only his appropriate share
As David's son endured, but greater load,

Taken from his o'erburdened countrymen,
Who, seeing there such godlike energy,
Piled on him the huge mountain of their woes,
All which he bore with patience in the strength
Drawn momently from power's exhaustless Fount,
The bosom of his Father, from whose trust,
Amid the wilderness of tangling cares,
Conflicting interests and rival claims,
Which form the battle-ground of human life,
Satan essayed to lure him, with the bait
Threefold, by which he long has kept the World
Dangling upon his hook. To appetite
He first appeals, unto ambition next,
And finally to fear; but all in vain
He plied his arts to draw that loving Soul,
From its firm anchorage, and send it forth,
Adrift on glory's phosphorescent seas,
In selfish quest of joy. Behold, instead,
The meek and faithful son, the brother kind,
The generous neighbor, the instructor wise,
And the renowned physician who relieves,
With tender hand, the sorrows of a race,
And ask no other fee but thanks to God.
Ah! what were all the thrones of Jupiter
To such dominion over Selfishness,
The devil that doth most afflict mankind?
Then stood revealed the Son of God, distinct
Above the blushing throng of heroes bald,
And demigods, that long had swayed the Earth
And won its blind applause. New light that hour

Dawned on the World, and through its dusky vales
And taper-lighted streets began to move.

But while the Son of God behind the veil
Of his enshrouding manhood wrought, concealed
In part, in part made known, by his rude mask,
His followers to some external heaven
Their thoughts directed, from ambitious dreams
Of glory and preëminence, of power
And vengeance, unconverted. Deeper yet
The renovating flame of love divine
Must penetrate, until the very roots
Of sin and weakness are consumed; till Self
Lies prostrate in the dust, and only God,
Dwelling in all his works, as in a house
Not made with hands, is worshipped: until then,
The stoutest heart will quail before the blast
Of warring elements that ever beat
Around the narrow isthmus between death
And life, to winnow well the golden grain.
Mark how the boldest of that stricken band,
On whose pale lips the extreme pledge of love
Was not yet cold, bowed like a hollow reed
Before the tempest, when sustaining grace
Was but a moment from his heart withdrawn.
But when the loving Saviour, taking hence
The shadow of himself, himself did give
To be the meat and drink of those he loved,
By inward virtue to the soul revealed,
They who but yesterday, like timid sheep,

Fled from their Shepherd's side, to-day, more bold
Than lions, calmly front the raging throng,
Or frowning judgment seat, ready, like Him,
To seal their testimony with their blood.
Thus from the ashes of a blighted World
Upsprings a fairer Earth, a sweeter Heaven,
Wherein dwells Righteousness from the pure root
Of love unfeigned arising—love to God
Incarnate in the love of Man—not there
Confined, but heavenward rising to its Sire,
Indissolubly joined with Him whose life
Pervades both Heaven and Earth, Soul of our Soul,
Light of our light, whose Spirit, through faith's root
Admission gaining, rises up and flows
Through every faculty, blossoms in love,
And burgeons in the fair expanse of thought,
Author and partner of the soul's deep joy.

Say then, fond muse, how fared it with our Dove,
After her lofty nest by the rough winds
Was twice unseated? Then beneath the Rock,
Upon the very ground, she fain would build,
Unwilling more the storm to tempt. At first
You should note nothing;—a few broken twigs
Lay cross-wise here and there—at intervals
Another added; then a little moss,
Which the kind Rock let fall, was loosely cast
Amid the pile. At length they shifted round
To a rude circle, and a tuft of wool,
Plucked by the envious hedge, was pressed between

The angles. Feathers next from moulting doves,
Or such as fell beneath the hunter's aim,
Were added; then a little down—and thus
Warmer and softer grew her bed, till, when
The woods were boisterous, she could steal away,
And find in her snug cleft a little rest.

Faint not, Pilgrim, Jesus guards thee,
　Watches o'er thee with an eye
Mild and tender as the rainbow,
On the flying cloud of summer,
　Saying " All the wrath is by."

What though Jordan's raging torrent
　Rolled above thy trembling breast?
Since our Ark those waves divided,
Heaven's immortal Dove descending,
　Makes the broken heart His nest.

Think of sorrow's night no longer:
　Banished all its guilt and gloom,
Through salvation's crimson portals,
Lo! the Bridegroom of the Morning
　Floods the blushing soul with bloom!

Who is this that comes from Edom,
　Godlike, o'er the cringing wave?
This with garments red from Bozrah,
Glorious in His apparel,
　And omnipotent to save?

While with tears His feet we cover,
    Kiss them, wipe them with our hair,
He our souls shall wash all stainless
In the Fountain of Bethesda—
    In the Fount of Love and Prayer.

Hark! what heavenly music welleth
    From those lips in blessing blest—
"Come to me, all ye that labor,
And with grief are heavy laden—
    Come, and I will give you rest.

Take my easy yoke upon you;
    Bear my burden, it is light,—
'Tis my burden to believe me,
On my righteous arm reposing,
    And true love my yoke of might."

God be thanked for such a Saviour!
    God be praised for such a Son!
Gentle Shepherd, Thou hast won me—
From Thy fond, pursuing footsteps
    I no more will blindly run.

At Thy sacred feet reclining,
    Listening to Thy words of cheer,
All my sins and woes forgotten,
All my empty trusts forsaking,
    Only Thy sweet voice I hear.

Loving much, as much forgiven,
    Lead me to our Father's throne,

Let me gaze upon His glory,
Feed me with Thy truth and beauty,
Make me all Thine own, Thine own.

Then Love's willing angel send me
Where the hungry sigh for bread,
Where the weary, captive spirit
On the thorny couch of conscience
Pillows her despairing head.

When Thy rod its work has finished,
Kindest then when most severe,
And she falls back on Thy bosom,
In her fainting heart I'll whisper,
"Now is thy salvation near."

IV.

As falls the April rain through boughs long bare,
Patters and trickles through the crisp, brown leaves,
And, without other answer, sinks away
Into the cool, rich earth, till, presently,
The sweet anemone her azure eye
Unlocks, with timid glance peering between
The rough fringe of the autumn's winding-sheet,
To see if Spring indeed be come again—
So fell Hope's warblings on a pensive heart:
There was a rustling of sad memories,
A stir of roots long bound with icy chains,
A secret swelling of the buds of hope,
And silence.
            God fears not that He should haste.
A day had closed in tempest; and a night
Of arctic length and gloom, changing from dun
To crystalline obscure, studded with stars
Whose beams were dagger-points, while the cold moon,
Like a weird sentinel, with measured step,
Trod round, at intervals, her icy beat,
Rolled slowly o'er her spirit. Gallantly,
While danced upon the wave one beam of day,

She had pressed onward, with heroic zeal,
To find an open passage 'twixt the dead
And living, or a sea by native warmth
Sustained. Into the icy jaws of Fate
She drove, till round her groaning bark they closed,
And made her soul a captive. In a world
Of darkness and of frost she learned how much
Of heavenly fire abides in human hearts,
When from the Sun of Righteousness they turn.

Slowly new morning dawned, in sober gray
Advancing, sign of prosperous end ; but cold
Over the snowy landscape shot the pale
Intelligential beams, in them no warmth,
But rather coldness visible,—whereat
We murmured not, remembering the storm
When day rose ruddy. Cautious over much,
I doubt not, we avoided paths once found
Disastrous, and with diligence pursued
What shifts for health or happiness Time brought,
Who fumbled all his pack, with goggled eyes,
Held up his wares and gilded ornaments,
And cried his trumpery, admiring much
He could find nought her either need to suit.

While thus employed striving to quench the flames
Of civil discord in her suffering form,
And wondering whereto the late providence
Might point, anon, as with the lightning's flash,
God rent in twain the gilded veil which masked
With lying shows of liberty and peace,

A virgin nation's like infirmities,
And on the world's careening stage led forth
The actors in a grander tragedy!

Mysterious Muse who, to my wondering eyes
Holding the mirror of lustrous life,
Instructest me therein with awe to read
The story of a race by sin enslaved,
By grace divine redeemed; attune my harp
To sing the rising theme, and show the bond
Of high analogy which links the past,
Present and future, things of earth with things
Above the earth, attesting God supreme
Over life's twofold realm. With his left hand
He shapes the growth of nations, while his right,
Upon the wreck of empires, thrones and states
Grown proud and tyrannous, or in the womb
Of their protecting orders, nourishes
That supermundane Kingdom which, ere long,
Will resurrect their broken forms, or change
Them living into new and nobler types
Of that Celestial Commonwealth where Love
With Liberty presides. Whence then the strife
Which shook with mortal throes a virgin Realm
And drove her from the golden gates of Peace
Into war's howling wilderness?—What cause
The contest urged when, maddened to his fall,
Oppression's Dragon with his sinuous tail
Drew down the third part of Columbia's stars
In foul revolt, plunging a continent

Beneath the crimson deluge of God's wrath,
And pouring men, like nitrous grains, incensed,
Into the belching hell of civil war?

When from the seeds of Liberty and Light,
By persecution's storms from the broad oak
Of Reformation scattered o'er the waste—
Exiles for conscience sake, in hungry quest
Of Freedom's bread and air with which to sing
God's praise—a sturdy and truth-loving race
Had sprung—the jealous British Pharaoh then
In harsh colonial bondage strove to bow
The Israel of nations. Long he bore
The hot indignity till God at length
His groanings heard, and, with an outstretched arm
And a high hand, from Egypt led his People,
In Revolution's bloody sea baptized
To Freedom, Justice and Fraternity.

Soon through the wilds of their transition stage
They took their march, led by the shining hand
Of Providence, and fed with wisdom's dews,
Their several Tribes ere long in one firm band
Cemented by a solemn covenant,
Distinguishing, in members manifold,
One organism of United States,
After the perfect pattern seen above,
Where the great stellar hierarchies join
Their shining ranks and orders infinite,
Obedient to a universal Code,
In one vast Empire, one broad Realm of Light,

Where Liberty and Law, in wedded walk
Bring forth the heavenly harmonies, and build
The stable mansions of enduring peace.

To fashion such an empire here below,
On pillars of Eternal Justice based,
God set his hand, but while his finger wrote
In secret on thought's radiant mountain tops,
The People, slipping faith in Righteousness
And Freedom, bowed before their Golden Calf—
To Slavery and Carnal Policy
Bending the supple knee. "These be thy gods
O Land of Liberty!" they cried, and joined
In merry dance around their brave Device,
Hastening to rivet on the hapless slave
The fetters wrenched from their harsh stepdame's grasp.
Soon to another tune they marched, soon drank,
In tears, Oppression's bitter dust, which bred
Intestine conflicts and became thenceforth
A deadly poison in the nation's blood,
Working far down beneath the seeming flush
Of health and beauty to corrupt the streams
Of honor, righteousness and faith. Full hot
The contest raged, threatening with utter ruin
The life of that apostate Commonwealth:
But interceding love prevailed, at length,
To win from God a respite of the doom
Inevitably that day sealed. The Law
Engraved on tables mutable, by man
Prepared, safely within its Golden Ark

Reposed, and in the Tabernacle framed
By human industry and skill divine.

Onward they moved beneath Heaven's sheltering cloud,
Spreading their tents afar o'er mount and plain;
But when in prospect of the final triumph
Of Universal Liberty they stood,
The dust of that base idol turned their feet
From Freedom's golden gates and warlike toil
Back to the howling wilderness. Pursued
By haughty Amorites they fled, nor staid
Their march, till almost to Egyptian bondage
And infamy returned. Twice forty years
From their approach to Liberty's fair shores,—
Repeating sin and doubling its account,—
They wandered in the dismal wilderness
Of sectional animosity and strife,
Where Korah lifted his rebellious head,
Sowing dissensions, and fire, dearth and plague
Wasted at noonday, till the very springs
Of Freedom ceased their flow, and the strong arm,
Chosen to shield the weak and innocent
From the oppressor, laid redoubled blows
On Liberty's grieved breast, commanding men
Formed in God's image to forget their rank,
And turn slave-hunters for the nation's foes.

Then from the riven Rock poured forth fresh streams
Of spirit-stirring eloquence, whereof
Both all the people and their cattle drank,
Until that ignominous flight was changed

To a more sure advance. But from that hour
Death waved his sceptre over the doomed state
Whose Law and Government unworthy proved
To lead the hosts of Freedom to their rest.
Wherefore God smote them with a breach, and called
The Higher Law of Justice, Truth and Right,
Ordained in Heaven, to be His People's guide,
And a fit chief and standard-bearers chose—
A Joshua indeed, o'er diffident
Of his appointed task, till thrice the Lord
And People cried, " Be strong ! lead on ! be strong ! "
Then firm and faithful as a rugged oak
That on some breezy height, conspicuous
Above the smoke of battle, calmly fronts
The molten storm, and waves its country's flag,
Till victory's eagle perches on its boughs,
When a stray shell from the retreating foe,
With envy charged, severs its noble trunk,
And lays its honors with the martyred brave.

So led, the youthful host of Liberty
Moved on, nor backward turned, till Freedom's Ark
Touched Jordan's foaming waves, when lo ! where seemed
No way of progress through opposing bounds
Of law and judgment, suddenly the floods
In wrath divided, leaving ample space
For the slow-moving columns to advance,
And bear to triumph through the open grave
Of dissolution, the Immortal Cause
Of Freedom, Justice and Humanity.

But only half the mighty task is done.
The harder part remains—to circumcise
The heart of a great nation from the blot
Of its iniquities and consecrate
Freedom's polluted Temple to its high
And sacred offices, ordained by Heaven
To be a Refuge for the desolate,
An House of Prayer and Praise for all the oppressed.

Now pours the costly chrism on a Land
Reeking with bondmen's and mother's tears!
The cup of her iniquity at last
Brims o'er!—rank blasphemy its fatal seal
Fixes on Treason's heaven-defying front!
The stone chosen of God is set at nought,
And an apostate temple boldly reared
On the dark mire and sands of Slavery!
Loose the four winds, O Angels!—from the North,
East, West and South, gather the scowling clouds,
Freighted with thunderbolts and battering hail,
Reserved against the day of wrath! Make broad
Destruction's wings! for not the Sunny Climes
Alone are guilty—the whole Head is sick,
And the whole Heart is faint;—both Government
And People have joined hands, in impious league,
To bind the chain upon God's helpless poor;
Now let them join, perforce, to loosen it,
Led by a Master's hand. What gratitude
To man is due, still faithless, seeking still
An earthly rather than a heavenly crown?—
For who in Freedom's trembling court or van

Dares yet strike boldly for the topmost cause
Of Universal Brotherhood? For Law,
Security and Union, to the storm
They fling the Patriot Banner, leaving God,
Through His accustomed ways, dark and profound,
To lead their footsteps to a loftier goal!

On mountain, shore and plain, through wood and vale,
O'er seas and the sea-swelling arteries
The burning vengeance wasted! Granite walls
Fell prone before the soul-dividing blast
Of thunder-throated trumpets belching doom,
And walls of flesh rolled down before the scythe
Of the Great Reaper on his iron car.
Death staggered with his burden, and the Grave
Sickened of royal diet! Brazen isles,
Floating invulnerable through Hell's red jaws,
Like risen Titans scoured the fated coast,
And from volcanic bowels spouting, showered
Comets and earthquakes and hot thunderbolts,
Till tattered cities bent their bleeding knees
And plead for mercy! Night grew hideous
With howling meteors, from the fiery hair
Of Mars shook off, that, like a thousand fiends,
Shrieked o'er the doomed and trembling capitols
Of rebel states, till, bursting from beneath,
Capped with the lurid ghosts of dying fanes,
A billowy sea of fire lashed the red wings
Of the retreating Darkness. Wide and deep
The bloody scourge invaded, making search
For the rebellious core; but, hydra-like,

Still round his lair the scaly monster rolled,
From flaming mouth and eyes defiance flashed
On Freedom's toiling armies, or swept back
The battle's living waves, and in his harsh
And torturing folds his hapless victims ground!

Why stand the hosts of Liberty at bay?
Or backward fly, frantic with maiden fear,
Before their puny foes, so late despised?
Why waste in fruitless dashes such array
Of might and valor as, in Freedom's cause,
Should breast a frowning World? Have they too spared
The Accursed Thing which a just God has doomed
To swift destruction? Ah, dissembling Nation!
There is an Eye which penetrates thy sin,
And will reveal thy poverty and strength!
" Deck now thyself with majesty and beauty!
Array thyself with excellence and glory!
O fair and puissant Virgin! cast abroad
The fury of thy wrath! look on the proud
And bring him low! the wicked in their place
Tread down, and bind their faces in the dust
Together! then will I confess to thee
That thy right hand can save thee!"
        Vain, all vain
Those gallant struggles while that secret sin
Lurks in her tortured breast! A devil armed
With mortal sting, sits like an incubus
Upon her panting bosom, draws her breath,
And twines his tightening coil around her soul!
Dizzy with circling marches, half entranced

By some mysterious spell, prone on her couch
Of agony, at the grave's mouth she lies,
Inebriate with her dream of liberty
And self-redemption by the stalwart arm
Of her own virtue, or in blank despair
And dumb amazement lost !
                              Then Israel
Bowed low before the Lord, and honor gave
To His potential Name, acknowledging
God only glorious, in whose regard
The nations of the Earth are but as dust,
The fine dust of that balance in which Truth
And Equity are weighed before His saints,
And found more pondrous than a thousand states,
With pride inflated, or by cruelty
Made odious in His sight.
                         Up ! Joshua,
And quit thee like a man ! No longer trust
In strength of mortal arm, nor longer plead
With empty hands, but load the rising prayer
With honest penitence, and mercy shown
To the oppressed, and justice to the foes
Alike of God and man ! Stretch forth the arm,
Power-girded, of a living faith, to save
A gallant nation from the blinding curse
Of Slavery ! Give to the instant flames
That ruthless monster which so long has spoiled
Freedom's fair heritage, laid waste her strength,
Defiled her glory, and, at last, with tears
Of blood, deluged a weary continent !

'Tis done! Now Glory be to God on High!
And on Earth Peace!—when the abating storm
Of war has done its work! Lo! as the Dove
Goes fluttering forth from Freedom's rolling Ark,
Bearing the Mandate of Deliverance
To a down-trodden People, from his seat,
High on God's finger perched, waiting the sign,
Down swoops the Golden Bird of Victory,
And hastens where the waves of battle roar
Round Freedom's trailing flag! Ere long the winds
Shift to the north, and with convergent weight
Sweep down the crested billows! The strong arm
Of the fraternal North is firmly drawn
Around the brave and beauteous South, fast bound
In the Oppressor's toils! The grizzly jaws
Of War begin resistlessly to close
Around the writhing Monster, till, at last,
In one terrific blaze, his prostrate length
Sinks hissing down beneath Hell's roaring flood,
While joyful millions cloud the heavens with thanks,
Whereon, as in celestial chariots, rise
To constellated mansions of renown,
The raptured spirits of the Patriot Dead!

Purged now of inward as of outward bonds,
Up Canaan's flowery hills, with modest step,
The resurrected Empire of the Free
Shall take her march, on deeds of glory bent,
Above renown and the vain glare of arms,—
To captivate, with the resistless might
Of virtue and beneficence, the hearts

Of kings and peoples, winning them from strife,
Envy and self-aggrandizement to deeds
Of Christlike chivalry, and arts divine,
Of peace and love, till, to her utmost bounds,
The ransomed Earth shall own fair Freedom's sway.

Hail, radiant Star of Dawn! chosen of God,
With thy auspicious sign, to lead the van
Of Freedom's Golden Age! Hail, Virgin Queen
Of Nations, twice baptized to keep the law
Of Liberty and Justice! Fairer now,
In thy humility, when from the shades
Of dissolution and of judgment drawn,
Than when ambition's laurels chilled thy brow,
Go meekly on thy course, trusting no more
In human strength or skill, but in the Arm
Omnipotent of Righteousness and Truth
And all-prevailing Love, whose golden yoke
Shall henceforth bind thee in fraternal league
With sister States and Empires nobler grown,
Through thy benignant ministries. The cross
For yet a season thou shalt bear, weighed down
By the sore fruits of disobedience,
While on thy sympathizing breast are laid
A World's vast sorrows—all the gathered ills
Of suffering Humanity, what time
The poor and the oppressed of other lands
Flock to the free and bounteous shores! All hail!
Sweet Land of Promise! To the bowing heavens
Thy golden mountains lift, with honor clothed,
As with a saintly robe, and o'er the seas,

Wave thy celestial Banner in all winds,
Proclaiming Liberty, man's birth-right, won
For each of Adam's exiled, wandering race
That cools his brow beneath the starry Flag
Of Freedom, Justice and Fraternity!

Hark! as the lightning from shore to shore
Flashes abroad the solemn warning,
Mountain and plain with its thunders roar
And glitter with mailed adorning!
Up! for the dream of peace is o'er!
Freedom hath grasped her sword of might!
God of battles defend the right,
And hasten the brighter morning—
When the strife of sword and tongue shall cease,
And the Lord of Hosts reign Prince of Peace!

Flag of the Free, once more unfold
Proudly thy galaxy of wonder!
And tell the tale thou hast ever told
In the battle smoke and thunder!—
Strong is the arm, and the heart is bold
That marshals 'neath thy conquering light,
To strike for the cause of Truth and Right,
And cleave the wrong asunder!—
And hasten the day when war shall cease,
And the Lord of Hosts reign Prince of Peace!

Land of the brave and noble-born!
Land of the mountain, plain and river!
Ne'er be thy locks of glory shorn,
By the hand which thee would sever!

From Evening's gates to the sunny Morn
Through all thy breadth let Justice dwell,
And Freedom's God shall guard thee well,
 And bless thy name forever!—
And the wrong and the woe and the strife shall cease,
And the Lord of Hosts reign Prince of Peace!

Salem of Rest and Liberty!
 Fair is thy seat on pleasant waters!
Kings thy nursing-sires shall be,
 And queens shall rear thy daughters!
Lengthen thy cords from sea to sea!
Strengthen thy stakes!—they come! they come!—
Earth's houseless wanderers are hastening home,
 Weary of bonds and slaughters!—
Here let the conflict of ages cease,
And the Lord of Hosts reign Prince of Peace!

V.

O DAY of Hope and Prophecy! long sought
With fainting eyes, and but in vision seen!
How many times shall the soft-rolling wheels
That bring thee toward this Arctic Zone retire,
With but a widening twilight for each age?
Six times have Eve and Morn alternate held
Millennial course o'er this degenerate Ball,
Which the Omnific Word is laboring
To recreate,—feeble, at first, the dawn,
Ere long in thick and palpable darkness quenched;—
All save a solitary star of hope
In the preserving Ark of Mercy borne,
Floating above the sullen sea of death.
At each vast revolution broader grew
The auroral radiance, until the Sun
Touched the horizon on the fourth glad morn,
But sank, ere long, behind the frigid mass
Of glacial humanity. At length
The rising glory spread into the North,
And tinged the Old World to its farthest bound,
O'erflowing westward, where, amid the wastes
Of a New World, trodden by savage men,

God had prepared a garden, round enclosed
By sea and mountain barriers, and, within,
Watered by four great river-systems,—one
To westward, compassing the Land of Gold,
To southward, one round Ethiopia poured,
A third bordering the winged lion's realms,
And flowing northward, while the fourth pursues
Southeasterly its course, and irrigates
The fertile slopes of that broad Paradise
Which the Lord planted on the eastern limb
Of Eden, with all trees of pleasant fruit
Adorned, and in the midst the Tree of Life,
Among the various goodly institutes
Preëminent, and, not far off, the tree
Of baleful operation, which bestows
Knowledge of good and evil—Policy.
Here the Creator, having brought the Man
Of godlike faculties and soul mature
For rational exercise, composed from all
The finer issues of each former age,
Commanded him to dress and keep the Land
For a perpetual heritage and home
Of Liberty and Love. Only huge beasts
Had Earth brought forth till now, chiefly intent
On prey and provender—self-interest
Their only law, acknowledged without shame
By men who call those nations and themselves
Christian! But works more worthy of that name
Shall soon be seen—nations in which the breath
Of the Creator shall infuse a soul
Of generosity, and godlike zeal
For justice and the general franchisement.

What here befel Heaven's offspring hath in part
Been shown—how Eve, by Satan's arts beguiled,
Tasted the fruit of Carnal Policy,
And saw her offspring rolled in guilt and blood :
How Adam shared her sin and punishment
Shall now appear as Thought, discursive, soars
Above the wilderness, where Zion's host,
Flying from stripes and bondage in the Old,
Their Land of Promise sought in the New World.

Lo ! scarcely had the lips of Deity
From Zion's mount proclaimed the sacred law
Of Freedom, Unity and Love,—one Head
Reigning o'er many members bound by faith
And brotherly affection in a free
And spiritual Body,—than the Tribes
Again bowed low before the Golden Calf,
Trusting by human righteousness and power
To gain their promised haven. Then the sword
Of the Dividing Angel from the cloud
Of God's enkindling wrath like lightning flashed,
Severing son from sire, and friend from friend,
Of all that rebel throng. Incompetent,
When to the very gates of Peace arrived
To enter Faith's inheritance through faith,
By fear and grief distracted, they returned
Into the waste and desolate wilderness
Of social anarchy, assunder cleft
In every member by the entering wedge
Of dissolution. Into Old and New,
Conservative, Progressive, Liberal

And Orthodox, they fell, still compassing
The mount of Carnal Ordinance, by fire,
Dearth, famine, pestilence and serpent fangs
Consumed. Full forty years their doleful march,
Under the sway of Moses, they pursued,
Learning the minor mandates of the Law,
Ere to his couch the stern Preceptor turned,
Leaving his task unfinished. But at length
God gave his rod to Joshua, transformed
Into a shepherd's crook, wherewith, e'en now,
The heavenly Leader gathers Zion's flocks
And scattered armies for a new advance.
And as the massing columns, rank by rank,
Emerging from the Wilderness, with songs
And hallelujahs greet the rising Day,
The cloud of God's mysterious Providence,
Touched with the rainbow tints of Charity,
Moves onward and condenses to a star,
Beyond the mists of Jordan, whose dark waves
Begin to blush, and swiftly fall away,
Before the Ark of Zion's liberties.

But what if Deep shall call to answering Deep,
And Heaven, like Earth, send forth its waterspouts?
What if those states in Zion most redeemed,
And joining to advance the sacred cause
Of spiritual enfranchisement, be met,
Mid way, by the confederated powers
Of darkness and oppression, bearing rule,
Through ignorance, o'er the deluded serfs
Beguiled to ruin by an Oligarchy

Of petty lords and tyrants, not content
With present sway, but eager to extend
The realm of bondage, till the kindling skies
Blaze with such strife as reddened earth of late,
When Freedom with her wily Dragon toiled?

Such conflict waits the militant Bride of Christ—
Whether with carnal or with spiritual arms—
Before her final victory o'er Pride,
Oppression, Avarice and Unbelief,—
As many as the populous tribes of Ham
That vexed the Promised Land, or rebel states
In Freedom's fair domain. But when the storm
Roars loudest, and the billows highest dash
O'er Freedom's trembling Ark, let Zion's hosts
Rejoice, for their deliverance is at hand!
Then shall it boldly be proclaimed that all
Who stand in God's fair image, whether Jew
Or Greek, Barbarian, Scythian, bond or free,
Are brethren, each of all, entitled thence
To suffrage in the councils of that State,
Whose Lord is the Elect of Earth and Heaven.
So shall the waves of strife increasing first
Their dying rage and strength, begin to fail.

Truth's burial is its planting in the soil
Of the blood-watered conscience. Thrice the Day
And Night weep over it, and lo! the grave
Is suddenly a shrine where emulous throngs
Pay rival honors to the star-crowned King,
Eternal, henceforth, and immortal known!

At midnight, when the New Jerusalem
Is compassed round with armies, when the World
Rejoices, and the saints in darkness weep,
When Sin grows bold, and Infidelity
Struts in the stolen garb of Truth, when love
Seems hate, and Reason grows irrational,
And the restraining arm of secular power
Must needs be added to the sober voice
Of Reason and Humanity, to save
Distraught Religion from the yawning gulf
Of dissolution, anarchy and strife,—
Then shall the joyful cry at last be heard,
"Behold the Bridegroom cometh with his Bride!"

Then shall the Lamb on Zion's top be seen,—
His chariot by a stalwart griffon drawn,—
Leading to final victory his hosts,
In twelve vast corps invincibly arrayed,—
An hundred four and forty thousand saints
That have not bowed before the Beast, or borne
His mark, but on their shining brows, instead,
The Father's name is written—the bright seal
Of life and immortality;—and fair
Above them in the roseate skies shall wave
The Starry Banner of the saints, emblazed
With Faith, Hope, Charity, the triune flame
Of heavenly Liberty's bright Morning Star.
So led, and in Truth's armor panoplied,
They shall advance, shouting the battle song
Of "Liberty and Union" till the walls
Of earth-defying Babylon, begirt

With the consuming fires of Love, and roar
Interminable of Truth's artillery,
Prostrate shall fall, amid the mingled shouts
Of angels and of men, to rise no more!

How long is theme for guessing this side Heaven,—
A task not wholly profitless perhaps,
Since thus the watchmen's eyes are kept alert,—
Unless while gazing upward to behold
The Son of Man descending from the clouds
Of an external heaven, we fail to note
His surer advent through the breaking mists
Of human ignorance and doubt, in light
Excelling Nature's glory.   Thus of old,
When Zion's hard-pressed legions strained their eyes
To see the archangel with his flaming torch,
Like a fierce comet with long, smoky train,
Sweep through the Empyrean to ignite
This withered Bog, behold, instead, all Hell
Broke loose and rushing on the frantic Church
Scattering her altars to the winds!   But lo!
'Mid disappointment and apparent wreck
Begins the expected miracle!   Each coal
Dashed in mad fury from Immanuel's shrine
Becomes a torch in the transparent hands
Of winged firemen, kindling where it falls,
In the dry grass of an idolatrous age,
Till the Old World in a red winding-sheet
Is wrapped, and from their worshipped seats in Heaven,
The Dragon, with his mythic deities,
Falls headlong to the howling deep.   From thence

He issued forth ere long in new attire,
As when, though once in the Red Sea o'erwhelmed,
He rose and followed after Jacob's sons,
A Golden Calf. Now from the sea he rose
A full-grown Beast, with seven usurping heads,
Armed with ten horns of persecuting power,
Wherewith he pushed the saints of the Most High
From their inheritance, and drowned the Earth
In darkness:—Truth and Reason were eclipsed,
And the World walked in grave-clothes 'mid the tombs
Of the Dead Ages!
      But while Death and Hell
Gloated in triumph o'er the horrid wreck
Of a world's blasted hope, Time struck the hour
Of morning watch, and straight a ruddy star
Rose like a rocket in the northern sky,
And like a bursting meteor flung its sparks
O'er half the hemisphere! Anon the flames
Of Reformation caught in the dry grass
And withered leaves, as when, in Autumn sere,
A locomotive roars along the vales,
Leading the train of Progress, and from forth
Its toiling furnace spouts contagious fire,
Which sends the ghost of the dead Year to Heaven,
Careering on the smoke of burning hills!
So the dry empire of the Latin Beast
Began to smoke along its northern front
When Michael placed the torch of Liberty
In Luther's stalwart grasp, denying works
Of imitation, or of man's conceit,
As purchase price of Heaven, whose single key,

Sufficient to command the golden bolts,
Is naked Faith, effectual through Love
To works of Righteousness. What wonder Rome
Bellowed with rage when this great corner stone
Of Liberty's fair Temple, without hands
From Zion's mountain cut, fell on the toes
Of the huge image of adulterous Power,
And they began to crumble, proving soon
They were but half iron and half potter's clay!

Dawn chases Night, and Evening treads on Dawn,
Wheel within wheel of being's spiral march
From darkness and inanity to God!
And so it came that the fell Beast whose head
Was wounded unto death, renewed his life,
With lengthened lease of power, and added sway,
What time protesting nations turned to lick
Their vomit, and impose their cast-off yoke
On riper protestants, till to the first
A second beast was joined, from the dry earth
Of sacerdotal pride and bigotry,
With lamb-like aspect but a dragon's voice,
From out whose minor horn issued a score
Of fragmentary and contentious sects,
Each bleating for a season with fair show
Of meekness, and loud cries for liberty,
Until, good footing gained, at once it wheeled
And pushed all non-conformists to the wall,
With a most catholic and puritan zeal
For undefiled religion.
      Virgin names
There are, written in gold in the Lamb's book,

Which are not blotted by the impious mark
Of the Oppressor. These upon their brows
Wore Love's celestial seal : but for the most,
Though faggot, ax and dungeon slowly fled
The rising day, Satan but changed his suit,
As he knows how, to fit the ruling mode,
Still plying his infernal rack and torch,
With sanctimonious zest, to heart and hope
And name. As finer grows the social warp
Finer he spins his woof, but still of goat
And leopard's hair, mingled with stolen wool
To hide the cheat.
     What differs whether Pope
Or Parliament, Court or Conventicle
Decree the pattern unto which the mind
Must cut its thoughts ? What matter, whether fire
Or malediction be the penalty
For looking through one's own eyes at the sun ?
Is it not persecution ? Veil thy face
Aholibah, Aholah is outdone,
For thou hast sinned against the greater light !
Hast thou not bowed to graven images,
And paid thy homage to a hundred saints ?
And in the name of Virgin Mother Church—
Still maculate, spite all the honors shown
By God and man—sought favor at Heaven's bar,
While nailing each new prophet to his cross ?
How augur'st thou that Rome is Babylon,
While thy self-righteous zeal is building high
The Babel of thy shame ? Enough has Rome
To wail for at the Grand Assize, but who

Shall stand as her accuser? Thou mayst learn
In Jordan's depths, ere then, to pity her,
And drop the stone from thy adulterous hand.

Know then that Babylon is *Mystery*,
The blindness of man's inner consciousness,
Who seeing truth but dimly through a veil
Of perishable forms, and deeming these
Part of the heavenly substance, jealously
Fights for their maintenance, as one who finds
His body threatened, and, in ignorance
Of its light value to the indwelling soul,
Defiles the diamond to preserve its case.
There Satan builds his stronghold, and from thence
Cannot be routed till man's spiritual eye,
By the long action of o'erbrooding light,
And Charity's balsamic anodynes,
Has grown so subtle as to penetrate
Each fading guise and see Truth face to face.
Hereto the ages tend, exchanging still
Ruder for finer symbols—stocks and stones
For altars and mysterious rites, and these,
At length, for verbal representatives,
Or letter types, that in the womb of Thought,
Imagination, form the needful eggs
Of Knowledge, which, by Truth's essential flame
Impregnated, brings the angelic birth
Of heaven-aspiring Sentiments and Thoughts.

Many stout daughters hath this haughty Queen
Who builds her cruel house in every land;
But paler grows its shadow to the west
Where Freedom's rival Empire brightest shines.
As when men speak of "Yankees" in New York,
They mean their neighbors o'er the Eastern line,
Southward, "those Vandals of the North," abroad,
This whole sharp-witted and industrious hive—
So Babylon to Englishmen means Rome;
To Puritans England holds rival claims;
Toward other non-conformists, Puritans
Knew how to play the beast with pious role;
And these in turn their heretics pursued,
With solemn frenzy of misguided zeal,
Till e'en those hornless lambs that loudest rang
The bells of Liberty, their lofty creed,
"God manifest in all," if any dared
Wed a fair "Gentile," wake the harp's glad soul,
Or but look on when "hireling priests" gave aid
At lover's leap, could gently join their heads,
And hoist them o'er the wall—for charity!
And when you rise at last o'er time's dark mists—
You that are hot in censure of these wrongs—
And wash your eyes in Canaan's crystal springs,
I doubt not such a cloud will be removed,
And fall back, like a mantle, o'er the world.
Your angel shall exclaim, "O, Babylon!
I too have been thy citizen, and helped
To build Oppression's towering walls, and rear
The hanging gardens of Self-righteousness!
But now, thank God, they are all fallen, fallen!

How long, O Lord, how long? Two thousand years,
Wanting a few, has the mysterious plea
Of thy Devoted One rung in thine ears—
"That they may all be one, as Thou in me,
Father, and I in Thee, that they may all
Be one in us." Alas, what mean those words?
For this have we been fighting many an age!
For this have poured out our brothers' blood,
And shed our own like rain, to make all men
Unite in one loud anthem to thy praise,
Without a jarring note to vex thine ear,
Or medley of discordant parts! But lo!
The more we struggle wilder grows the strain
With angry discords, till Thy Temple roars
With jargon such as scattered men of old,
When pride and infidelity combined
To build an earthen stairway to the skies!
What do we more, who strive with blood-stained hands
To build a Mansion for the Prince of Peace,—
Use anger for cement, and hate for gold!
Who stretch forth mortal hands unsanctified,
To stay that Ark which is the stay of worlds!
Who, having tuned our dulcimer and harp
To please our own ear, go about to break
Our neighbors' lute and cymbal!—if our throats
Pipe treble, will have lions pinch their lungs
To warble with the wren! Well have we tried,
O star-crowned Minstrel! what our hands can do
To mend the thunder-organ of Thy world,
On which Thy spirit, breathing peace or storm,

Brings forth such mingled melody our ears
Can scarce discern the air! Forgive! forgive!
And lend us grace and wisdom to expound
Our own, and leave to Thee the master's part!

"That they may all be one!"—ah! He said not
"Like one!" That were a doleful house indeed
Which had but one continuous honeycomb
Of cells, however filled with cloying sweets!
How tedious were the walks of Paradise,
If bordered all their length with banks of rose!
Only that robe is white in which the dyes
Of the seven great archangels sweetly blend!
Mark with what infinitely varied grace
God clothes his beauteous form in Nature's vest!
And would ye paint His Daughter like a mole,
Or a bronze statue? Hence! ye daubs, nor dare
To touch His darling with your whitewash brush,
And your unhallowed mixtures! In the heart
Dwells the true rouge, by love's quick chemistry
Prepared. Not all the creeds in Babylon,
With all the garnish on St. Peter's walls,
Can make the Bride of Jesus half so fair
As one sweet deed of humble charity!

If thou would'st have all men with thee agreed,
Agree with all. Who bade thee take this seat
Above thy brethren, and assume the guide
Of faith and conscience? If thou art our judge,
Show thy credentials. What! this mouldy scrip,

Soiled with the dust of ages? Did He say,
"By this shall all men my disciple know?"
What if thy father were an Abraham,
And thou a Judas? is thy bishopric
Inalienable? "If any will be chief,
Let him become a servant unto all."
Where then is Israel's lord? Were there not twelve
Born to one Father, all whom he did serve
As doth a mother, and bestow his life,
To prove that Love must rule by his own force,
And that true sovereignty dwells underneath
The governed, as the root beneath the tree?
"One Father, even God; one Master, Christ;
And many brethren peers:"—on this firm stone
Rests the broad Temple of man's Liberties,
And though the rains descend, and tempests roar,
And torrents thunder round its steadfast base,
Time's latest age shall see its crystal sheen
Expanding over continents and seas,
While resurrected states and empires free,
With homes innumerable of peace and love,
Securely rest beneath its ample dome!

Arm you, therefore, O Patriots of the Cross,
Who shrink not from such title to a crown,
But not with carnal weapons! If the foe
Invite the civil arm, that arm shall cure
His madness; but to you belongs the task
Of routing Principalities and Powers

Intrenched in servile ignorance and fear
And superstition, fortresses more strong
Than ancient Babylon's imperious walls !
Your gateway is the lowly river-bed
Of self-denying love. Go, turn aside
Euphrates, with a million humble acts
Of kind humanity, then enter in
Bearing the Banner of Redeeming Love,
Truth's two-edged sword, Faith's shield, and the breast-
    plate
Of Righteousness, defense more sure than brass,
Salvation's helmet, and upon your feet
Those golden sandals, Liberty and Peace !

As when an iceberg rolling from the coast
Of glittering, stark and cold formalities,
Encounters the Gulf Stream, and, with it, shower
Of tropic arrows from the noonday sun,
Soon the pent spirit in its pores begins
To ask more room ; spar after spar falls off,
Limb after limb breaks from the rigid mass,
And, melting, mingles with the joyous sea,
Whose free glad waves clasp hands around the world—
So shall Oppression's frigid walls dissolve
In the approaching summer heats of time !
Then shall come Love's espousals ; then all souls
Inspired with a divine benignity,
And crowned with Charity's celestial flame,
Shall flow into the vital harmonies
And free organic unities of Heaven !

To vitalize the void, phlegmatic mass
Of Nature, and her warring elements
Reduce to order, harmony and grace,
By the infusion of a nobler life,
Imparted from His all-creative Word,
Was God's first labor, then for rest exchanged
When her machinery, in order set,
Began to quiver to His tuneful breath,
And echo Heaven's orchestral melodies.
And when the crude, chaotic elements
Of dead Humanity, drinking from Christ
The spirit of obedience and love,
Shall from brute proneness rise to manly walk
Of self-poised liberty ; when rival states
And churches, belching long with envious rage,
Shall own the flame of brotherly regard,
Convert their cannon into railroad bars,
And the swift-flying messengers of hate
To telegraphic nerves and tongues of peace,
With which to bind their members into one
Consummate Manhood, ordering affairs
By counsel, and deliberative weight
Of judgment, in the common interest
Of Virtue and Humanity, again
The renovating hand of God shall rest
Upon His rounded shock of golden sheaves.

> Hark! from the Golden Mount above
>   Resounds the joyful trumpet's warning!
> See where the militant Bride of Love

Girds on her bright adorning!
Lo, where Heaven's immortal Dove,
Over the warring Lamb of God,
Fast where Freedom's hosts have trod,
Leads on the blissful morning,
When the strife of brother with brother shall cease,
And the Lamb long slain rule Prince of Peace!

Empire of Light, whose sister spheres,
All round a common center turning,
Backward have rolled Earth's golden years,
The lesson of faith while learning,
Wake! for thy bridal dawn appears!
Waving His Banner o'er land and sea,
With the torch of Love and Liberty,
Jesus the world is burning!
Now shall thy sons like the stars increase,
For Zion's Lord is the Prince of Peace.

Lo! where the New Jerusalem,
Fair as the Sun on a golden ocean,
Flames like a royal diadem
With love's divine emotion!
Twelve broad gates, and through each gem
Enter twelve nations chanting the psalm
"Glory to God! Worthy the Lamb
To receive a world's devotion!
Cease, O Time! let thy waiting hours cease,
And Eternity crown the God of Peace!"

VI.

METHOUGHT I heard an angel whisper "soon."
 O, who will tell us what means "soon" in Heaven?
"Soon, soon," the Warning Angel ever cries,
"He cometh who shall come." Men lift their heads,
Smile, half in hope and half in irony,
Breathe short, then long, take up the scythe and sword,
Go sweating, bleeding, staggering on. "Soon, soon
The Righteous Judge shall come, and shall not tarry,"
Breaks forth again, above their shouts and groans:
But fainter sounds the echo from beneath,—
As when a bugle blast, from hill to hill,
Leaps through the dreamy dark, and dies away
In the oblivious depths of slumbering woods.
Each generation hears the trumpet call,
And hastens toward Heaven's armory; but soon
Forgets to hope, forgets to fear, forgets
That to eternity all things are soon.

"The Son of Man so cometh as a thief
By night."—
    "Heard you that stealthy footstep, brother?"

"Where, dearest, on the street?"
"Nearer, I think:
Not farther than the porch."
"It may have been
The rustling of the Wind, who often sweeps
In silken robes through street and corridor,
And gently taps, or thunders at their doors,
To let men know there is a Spirit near
Who gives them all their breath, and will, ere long,
Recall His ill-used loan."
"Listen again!
It sounds within the hall."—
"I hear no step,
Nor deem it possible that one could pass
The bolted door so silently. Fear not."

"Well, read to me again."
"'If the good man
Had known what hour of night the thief would come,
He would have watched.'"—
"I think I heard a step
Upon the stairway leading to my room
Were I to lose my jewels it were sad.
Our mother gave them to me, and for this
I hold them dear, though, for heir proper worth,
I little value them."
"I will make haste
And see that all is well."
"O, brother, stay!
Thy life is more to me than all the gems

And glittering trinkets of the Vatican.
But make a noise and he will fly."
                           " And bear
Our precious mother's gifts."
                           " But what are they
To life ? I have outgrown the use of beads,
And bracelets are but fetters to my arms.
Go not."
            " But for our honored mother's sake,
And his who gave them to her, I esteem
No sacrifice in their defence too great."

" 'The life is more than meat '—and how much more
Than things which do but symbolize a love
So living that it can renew its types,
At will, while life remains. But this extinct,
What further value have those mocking gems ?
Yet, if thou wilt, my love shall go with thee
For thy defence."—
                  " He is escaped, and lo !
Thy casket here lies broken. O, my heart,
How had I rather parted with some drops
Of thy red anger, than beheld this woe ! "

" Alas ! the time is coming when the Thief
Thou readst of will more sorrow give than this,
But anger none. Ev'n now his stealthy foot
Is on the stairway leading toward the place
Where jewels more esteemed than these are kept.
Perhaps their solid value is no more,

In eyes that look beyond Earth's glittering shows,
And realize the substance of its dreams.
But oh! my heart misgives me! I have wrought
No worthy deeds to prove my love sincere.
In all things disappointed, nought remains
But a poor broken casket, from which all
The jewels have been stolen—all those gifts
And ornaments with which I thought to make
My spirit lovely in the eyes of Him
I would have called the Bridegroom of my soul.
But now I dare not utter the bold thought,
Or give it lodgement in my empty brain:
For when I would have beautified myself
With acts becoming one to honor called,
And sought his palace—not in arrogance,
As though the virtue were at all my own,
But with that ornament of greatest price,
Humility, shedding its crowning charms
O'er all the crown of heavenly gifts—amazed,
I could not lift one jewel to my hair.
But still I ceased not struggling, like the fond
And foolish Bride of Christ, who, in her zeal
To compass her own glory, thrust the sword
Into her bleeding bosom, and pulled down
The mountain crags on her ambitious crest.

Thus, in the blindness of my vanity,
I fought the battle with my own false heart
And treacherous ambition to the end,
And came forth vanquished, stripped of ev'n the grace

Which genial Nature gave. Yet, in due time,
Deep working mercy lifted from the dust
This shattered heart and brain, in which remained
But emptiness and some small faculty,
To hold new gifts of Goodness Infinite,
Which asks but opportunity to give,—
To pour abroad love's blissful radiance,
Freely, to rejoicing Universe.

This lesson, which my head knew long ago,
I trust I may yet learn by heart : but ah!
So little has been lent me of that Faith,
Whose vast capacities I once beheld
In vision, but so failed to realize,
And so much less have any worthy fruits
Appeared from that received, I tremble now
Lest when the Son of Man—and who is that,
But our mortality?—shall take away
The little residue of Nature's dower,
There shall be nothing left,—no inward germ
Of heavenly virtues, from the Son of God
Inherited, with which I may begin
The life eternal.
            Oh! could I but feel
The comforting assurance, of more worth
In such an hour than all ambition's toys,
That when the lapsing waves of this wild life
Shall leave my spirit on the star-paved beach
Of the eternities, the Gracious One
Will lift me up, and, like a new-born babe,

Tenderly fold me in His loving arms,
And kiss away my unreturning tears !
What then were all those pains which in my breast
Compel the stifled moan ? Then I should know
They were the travail-pangs of my soul's birth.
But with this cold vacuity, this doubt,
This yearning after love, which only falls
In dew-drops on the desert of desire,
How can my heart contend ?
       Have patience now,
For the pent tides are flowing, and the eye
Turns fondly to the mist-clad past, from which
The clouds begin to lift. My aching lips
Have long hushed thought's confusion, for no cause
Could I perceive for the entanglements
Which bound my feet when I essayed to scale
Heaven's golden mount, but my rare wickedness
In turning from my Shepherd's lead : for true
Those pointings of his luminous finger seemed ;—
Were doubtless true at first ; but when I shrank
From duty's onward path through infirm trust
In His omnipotence, inwardly leaning
Upon my own frail arm, God also turned,
In seeming wrath, knowing I was not ripe
For His divine employ. Then, sorely grieved
At my reverse of fortune—more concerned
For my own gain than my Redeemer's cause,
And the salvation of immortal souls—
Under the inspiration of my fears,
Rather than Duty and heart-strengthening Love,

I rallied, and made head against my foes,
Led by some Jack o' lantern, that rose up
To mock Truth's Guiding Star. The sequel all
May learn who strive to enter Paradise
By dint of human power—in whom death's fire
Has done but half its work, purging the heart
Of gross and flagrant sins, but leaving still
The roots of discord in the soul's dark depths.

Oh! brother, it doth often seem to me
That I have lived in vain, who hoped to live
A noble life, and something for my kind
Accomplish—something that should increase joy
And beauty in the Earth! It may be well:
For some seem born merely to be—to drink
The precious overflow of God's great love,
Which else would go to waste. And who can tell
But these are just as honorable deemed,
As dear to Him, who counteth very love
The topmost crown and blossom of our being,
As those in whom it works to form a seed
Of other loves,—save that in magnitude
The one excels the other? And perhaps
In the fair Coming Time, in the broad fields
Of Love's celestial Paradise, the flowers
Plucked early and unfruited from the Earth,
And grafted in that kindlier soil, may yield
A seed of all their charms and lovingness
To spring in other hearts, as angels spread
Their beauteous race, and fill the worlds with bloom.

Such visions sometimes flit across my mind,
Like angels' wings, throwing a gleam of Heaven
Into the darkness, and inspiring hope
That some fruition may at length arise
From my sore tutelage, when to my couch
Retired, happy if from some quiet nook
In Heaven, I may behold my Saviour's face,
And watch at distance life's tumultuous play,
Leaving to thee, perhaps, a double task,—
Unless my spirit still with thine may work,
And, one without, and one within the veil,
Together labor still to understand
The mysteries of human life, and shed
Hope's cheering radiance o'er its desert paths,—
Rewarded if some fainting pilgrim gain
Fresh courage from these foot-prints in the sand.

Faith's flickering lamp is shining brightly now,
Giving a moment's rest, but well I know
Darkness will come again, and Sorrow knock
At my heart's door, and easy entrance win ;
For mortal-bound immortal still is weak,—
Frail as the wind-blown gossamer, which clings
Fondly to its dead spire of sighing grass,—
And from the great Untried instinctively
Turns to this rude and melancholy world,
Still dear with all its frailties.
                                    When I flung
My maiden tresses 'neath that Juggernaut,
Whose wheels are fattened with the blood and brains

Of many of our country's noblest youths,
And fathers not a few—Intemperate Haste,
Our nation's scourge—how little did we dream
Of this sad ending to Ambition's race.
Then the thief entered at the vine-clad door,
Through which he visits many a happy home,
And lays its beauty waste ; and since that hour,
Smiling at our late vigilance, and all
The schemes of knit-browed Art, has roamed at will
Throughout this haunted mansion, robbing me
Of health, peace, comfort, joy and length of days.
"Mysterious providence!" it may be called,
But more like my improvidence it seems,
Still worthy of regret, however grace
May break or mend my fall. Pardon me then
If long and almost vain have been my struggles
For the becoming shroud of resignation,—
If still I cannot say that all is well,
While yet unfinished lies my morning task,
With mid-day's needful labors quite untouched,
And but half-learned my evening hymn.
        O, Earth!
How beautiful thou art with all thy woe!
Even with the blush of shame upon thy cheek,
Or war's dead hectic, thou art lovely still,—
Lovely to sight, though bitter to the taste,
And fairest when thy hand is most severe,
For then we fear to lose thy favors quite.
But I am well-nigh weary of thy frowns,
And ready to accept thy last embrace,

So it be gently given. Why should Death,
Now so familiar grown, appalling seem,
To one full long a playmate with his shadow,
When thousands, still untaught by lingering pains
To sigh for rest and shrink from its approach,
Rush to his arms with songs upon their lips,
And battle shouts rending the ghostly air ?

Alas ! my country, who shall stay the tide
Of our fast-ebbing life ? Alike in sin
And in its punishment, one only way
To rest and happiness for us remains—
The lowly pathway of the River's bed !
Peace to thy troubled bosom ! Peace, O, Peace,
For my impatient soul and weary frame !
And thou, unhappy Earth, and thou, O fair
And long-afflicted Daughter of the Skies,
May God, in tender mercy, give us Peace !"

——It was the latest sabbath of the year,
That year of strife and darkness, when a world
Anxiously watched the alternating scale
In which a gallant nation's life was laid.
As anxiously we watched a nearer strife,
In which were mirrored Time's last agonies.
Midsummer had brought hope : slowly her feet
Seemed rising life's green hills, fair with her smiles ;
But Autumn came, and with the falling year,
Her steps turned downward, nevermore to climb
The wearying heights of Earth. Then faithful Hope

Spread out her wings, and flew across the vale,
Sweeping a way through Jordan's brightening mists,
To where, in the dim azure, on the hills
Of Paradise, a Shepherd with his flocks
Seemed slowly this way tending. Sometimes clouds
Obscured the vision, and again it broke
With solace on the eye, as, step by step,
She neared the passes of the Silent Stream.

Nature was tranquil; on December's brow
The storm had spent its wrath, and left the World
Robed in a winding-sheet of innocence.
Alike on fruitful field and barren heath
Oblivious grace had fallen, sternly kind,
And Earth seemed once more cradled in God's arms.
The pensive beams of the declining Sun,
As if in fondness for the dying Year,
And the sweet flower he would bear with him, bathed
All Nature in a spring-like glow, and played
Tenderly round the sofa where reposed,
In seeming sleep our waiting Voyager,
Who, like a pure, pale water-lily, kissed
By sorrow's lapsing waves, began to fold
Her fragrant petals for the night. Not yet
Had perfect peace been given. Tremblingly
She saw the opening mouth of life's dim cave,
As when a miner leaves his dreary toils,
To seek the light of day and home's sweet rest.
But shrank with diffidence from Heaven's bright blaze,
Fearing lest it reveal some lingering stain

Upon her soul, displeasing to the eyes
Of Him whose love she craved.   Waking at length
From sleepless sleep she called me to her side,
And said with nature's sweet simplicity,
" I had a pleasant time when you were out ;
In my distress, with a more earnest faith,
I called on God ; He heard, and answered me
With the pure light of my Redeemer's face.
Sweet were the moments of that interview,
But oh ! it was so short ! "
       The Morning Star
Of Heaven's eternal Day thus rose and shed
Its radiance o'er her soul.   Then folding up
Her thoughts and smiles in calm, majestic peace,
She rested till the evening watch, when lo !
The Somber Angel stretched his fiery hand
And touched the silver cord ! the Golden Bowl
Lay broken,—dust was dust, and spirit Home !

No form, no sound, no motion ! all alone !
No voice, no glance, no smile answers my own !
There was a vision—it would not abide !
There was a presence—now there is a void !
I knew a joy—an aching now I feel !
Where flowed a rupture is a wound to heal !
Once there was music in life's ocean roar ;
Now the waves moan along a sighing shore !
I saw two friends life's flowering summit scale ;
I see a stranger wandering down a vale

*Alone! Ah, well, I will go in and stir
The ashes ;—God, no doubt, was kind to her.*

*Alone?—no, not alone!—the Pleasant One,
Who, ere Creation wakened, dwelt alone,
Yet not alone, is with me! Even He,
Primeval Sire, had pleasant company
In his own Word and Thought. In his vast soul
Life's mighty Embryo moved, wherein the whole
Of Nature, both the spirituous and firm,
Lay folded like an undeveloped germ,
Rolling and ripening in the Eternal Breast,
Whose bliss is action, and whose labor rest,
Till the Omnific Word, in radiant birth,
Began to pour Creation's glories forth,—
Angel and starry hosts, like sparks that roll
From pregnant Etna's beatific soul!*

*Alone? O, no! compassionate Saviour, Thou
Hast trod the path my soul is travelling now!
Thou knowest each rise and fall, each thorn and stone!
The footsteps which I ponder are thine own!
They too are streaked with blood, wherewith 'tis meet
That mine should mingle, while my lips repeat,
" Thy Will be done." Save in the paths of sin,
I cannot go where thou hast never been ;—
Can find no rock not softened by thy tears,
No cave so dark but there thy lamp appears:
This aching heart bereft of answering love,
This spirit moaning like a mateless dove,*

This weary eye and brain, whence light has fled,
This heaving bosom and stone-pillowed head,
Far more than I can name, thou knowest them all—
The vinegar, the wormwood and the gall!—
Rejected by the world thou camest to save,
No refuge from thy people but a grave,
When timid friends, like summer birds, were flown,
Though man-forsaken, thou wert not alone!
But when thy Father's righteous judgments, hurled
In dreary darkness o'er a wicked world,
Veiled from thy sight His face— O, tender Heart!
That sword went through thee—from thy God to part!
Now thou canst pity us, whom sin beguiles
So often from our Father's blessed smiles,
And death long weary years from them divides,
Whose going taketh from us all besides!
But grief is no more grievous when thy lip
Touches with ours in sacred fellowship;
Nor sorrow sorrowful when thy warm breath
Uplifts the soul, and exiles woe and death!
Fragrant with odors of celestial spring,
I feel it blowing o'er me while I sing,
Till, borne on angel's wings, I mount the sky!
Where is thy sting, O, Death? where, Grave, thy victory?

Alone! What lights are these which round us burn?
Do Moses and Elijah too return?
When the Good Shepherd visits those they love,
Do his saints linger in their fold above,
Or come they also on cherubic wings,

Where Love immortal to her birthplace clings?
Perhaps they aid to bear the gift He brings;
Perhaps their harvest in our thoughts they reap;
And oft, I ween, they sooth us when we weep,
And tender vigil o'er our slumbers keep :—
Fond mother bending o'er her infant's rest;
Kind father blessing those he oft has blessed;
Sweet sister twining flowers of heavenly bloom
Round brows that faithful beamed through joy and gloom;
Or brother, with seraphic tenderness
Soothing dark anguish with love's soft caress;
The child of many prayers eager to bring
To broken age its grateful offering;
Or soul espoused for life's congenial tie,
And bound through death by that which cannot die,
Returned with balm from love's celestial bowers,
To shed delight on sorrow's darkest hours :—
O, stars that ever with the shining Sun,
Mingle your beams, and when a day is done,
And He retires to let your light be seen,
Pour your soft smiles from the o'erbrooding sheen
Of your eternal resting-place—by name
I know you, gentle friends! The sacred flame
Of your sublime benevolence, I feel,
As often through life's solitudes ye steal
Around my heart, to fan the languid fire
Of its devotion, and awake desire
To loftier aims, and hope's bright garlands weave,
And whisper to my soul, " Believe, believe!
Though Earth be dark, O bright is heavenly day!

Though blinding grief, a moment ends its sway!
Though hard thine earthly couch, there is a Breast
Where weary spirits may forever rest,
Their hunger all appeased, their warfare done,
Woe ever ceased, joy ever but begun,
To drink with us, in glittering courts above,
Immortal streams of beauty, light and love!—
No more of grief, no more of loneliness,
But one vast chorus of unbounded bliss!"

VII.

BEHOLD yon beauteous Planet, O my friend!
   Which seemed to melt into the gold of heaven,
But perished not from love's attentive gaze.
Ev'n when the Sun has risen we can feel
Its placid beauty shining from the depths
Of its ethereal home, as if to say,
What more is death to the immortal soul,
Than its unrobing from the shades of night?
What thinkest thou? may loving hearts perceive
The subtle radiance of kindred fires,
That have put off their mortal covering?"

"Truly it seemeth not impossible."

"Why, when the stilling hand of Death has closed
The lively senses to our fond appeal,
And the reluctant, solemn sepulture
Has borne the precious ashes to their rest,
Does the bisected heart sometimes defy
The arrow-point of grief, still beating joy
Through all the soul, as if the arteries
Through which the purest of its pleasures flowed,
Were still unsevered—still aflame with life,
And sweet reciprocal love, outlasting death?"

"It argueth continuance of the Dead
In occupation of their native sphere,
Or, that our sense of their late presence with us
Is still so vivid that it doth impress
Our spirits with a like regard of them.
Truth has so many substances and shadows
Of nice resemblance, 'tis most difficult
To draw the line between what seems and is."

"Hence she doth labor to procure for us
A twofold witness, Consciousness and Sense,
Grounding our intuitions in a form
Of tangible effects, to indicate,
Past doubt, the verity of that conceived,
And Thought's ethereal features more define.
To me the world contains no stranger thing
Than that, if disembodied spirits live,
They cannot make their presence known to us
By some indubitable proofs, but mope
And shadow round us, leaving us to guess,
From the uncertain longings of the soul,
And tedious arguments of no more force
Than serves to keep the fluttering breath in Hope,
At questions of most infinite concern,
Which one clear glance would set at rest."

       "And then
Another would be wanted, and another,
'Till we should have no patience with our life
In this dull world, where our chief business is

Until the shell be broken of that egg
From which our struggling angel must be hatched.
Perhaps it is enough for our best weal—
For the development of moral nerve
And fiber, which have ever flourished best
In temperate climes—that we imbibe the warmth
Of God's o'erbrooding spirit, ignorant
For a few days of the celestial walks
Of being, and what fair wings flit around
And chant their gladness in the open sky."

"The figure is well chosen, but methinks
The shell about our souls is growing thin,—
Tender almost to rottenness. A touch
Will break it now which but a few years since
Had harmless proved; and haply, for this cause,
'Tis more translucent now than formerly,—
Though in all ages there have not been wanting
Some of more delicate nerve, whose subtle organs
Distinguished shadows of celestial forms
Through life's attenuate veil. Why should the World
Go ever muffled in the swaddling clothes
Of infancy? or wearing bonds of youth?
Have the paternal Skies no waiting dower
Of freedom and fresh knowledge for its manhood?—
Nought for Midsummer, to the budding spring
Denied?—nothing for Autumn's thank-day feast,
Or Winter's cheer reserved?"

" To these belong
The fruits of the spring sowing, both of sin
And virtue ; all the trees in Eden planted
Yield their due increase ; but the Tree of Life—
The witness of his immortality—
Was hid from man when his incontinence
Led him to grasp at things beyond his reach,—
Seeking to be a god before his time.
If from the innocent a Father's love
Would keep excess of knowledge, wherein lies
No little peril to the unripe soul,
With how much care should a sin-blighted world,
Lost to an inward conscience of the truth,
Be guarded from the serpent's glozing tongue?
For it may prove that all who speak as gods
Are not of God, but use the tongue of beasts,
Or some like instrument of magic art,
With purpose to delude the credulous,
And lure the mind from an internal lead,
And spiritual communings, to depend
On outward signs which bring no certain proof
Of truth, or spiritual identity."

" Yet, granting the inherent poverty
Of matter, whether animate or dead,
Fitly to image truth so that no lie
Can hide beneath it, still we must believe
That God intends it for some honest use.
Whether esteemed the base or shadow of being,
Its value reaches to the highest heaven.

Jehovah's self despised not its embrace,
And promised further honors in the future,
When to the World He gave His Well-Beloved;
And if aught evil have crept into it
For our seduction, would it not seem wiser—
More Christ-like—with a whip of righteousness,
Faith and intelligence to drive it out,
Than weakly to abandon our just title
To all Truth's fair domain ? If Mother Eve
Let in so bad a guest, that for a time
The angels were ashamed to visit her,
Unless they wore a veil, she had a daughter
So credulous toward God that He disdained not
To greet her with a lover's kiss, so fervid,
That from that hour the sluggishness of matter,
Opaque through sin, began to pass away,
Giving some ground for hope that finally
The correlated powers of Consciousness
And Sense will grow so subtle and refined,
That their joint operation will reveal
The substance of our dim imaginings ;
And being's inner sanctuary expose
To reverent inspection,—laying bare
Heaven's long-kept secrets. To what purport else
When on the cross Messiah's flesh was parted
Was the like symbol in the Temple rent
From top to bottom !—mark you, *from the top
Unto the bottom !* which doth signify,
That the obscurity shall be removed
First from man's higher nature, but at length,

Through the redeeming sympathy which joins
Body and soul, his lower powers shall share
The blessed vision of celestial life."

" It would indeed appear that until then,
The Great Reformer hath not perfected
His enterprise. But for this consummation,
Mankind must wait till Death has had his due
For Heaven's infracted law. When Earth and Sea,
Shot through with lightnings of His countenance,
Give up their dead, as did the Sepulchre
Its slumbering Lord, then shall these hidden powers
Resume their native functions, opening wide
Our doors to heavenly visitants."

"Behold !
Out of the mist-clad Deep they rise ! The dead
Are no more dead ! in forms of living light,
Substantial, incorrupt, the ravished Grave
They quit, and stand before the throne of God
For judgment. All things perishable, false
And vain shall now be given to the flames ;
Truth, Wisdom, Righteousness to glory rise,
Eternal in the Heavens ! Why should our sight
Be ever fixed upon the blinding dust
Of carnal images ? What portion, pray you,
Of man's decaying body is reserved
To seal his dubious identity,
If in the living soul the key be wanting ?
Of all the garments which the spirit weaves

And yearly casts away, which must the Earth
Surrender ere the sons of God can spread
The feast of immortality? Why join
Things most unlike to prove that literal
Whose essence only is of solid worth?
Did Jesus from the grave his ashes take,
When but a thimble-full remained, and call
The winds, the sea, the flower, the rock to give
Their stolen treasures back to Him, and then
Compose the selfsame shadow of Himself
Which on the Cross was broken? Did not Love
Paternal rather keep that golden type,
To show by its uplifting that the grave
Had lost its power to mar what filial trust
In God makes incorruptible? Such form
Within the outer garments of his flesh
Hath man, as the devouring worm and fire
Of Nature's searching inquest cannot touch,
While by a more celestial form sustained,
In which the flame divine of God's own life,
Abides. In such a form the angels dwell,
And, as they need, lay hold of nature's powers
To work God's will, as men attire themselves
In woven vestments, whether new or old,
As suits their company or toil—of life
An adjunct, not a part. What if the Lord
Of Earth and Heaven should to His Angels say,
"Prepare anon your mighty armament
For the concluding act of our long war
Against Idolatry and Unbelief,

The two grand foes that now on either hand
Assault our kingdom in the Earth with din
Of noisy and conflicting arguments !
Go therefore and prepare our final siege
At once of Rome and Athens !"—what I say
Should hinder the rejoicing hosts of Heaven,
Who at His bidding sway this lower world
And hold in check its stormy elements,
From gathering round their pure celestial forms
A luminous vestment of the finer threads
In Nature's loom, to signal to mankind
The coming storm, as when the weather-gods,
With shining shield and spear, deploy their ranks
In ominous glory all across the north
By night, and sometimes in the zenith wave
The crimson flag of elemental war ?
'Tis said clear-eyed observers have already
Caught glimpses of the vanguard hastening
To break the ground, and fill the yawning trench,
And plant the cannon. Doubtless Doubt should stand
At Reason's side what time she doth inquire
Of things so marvelous, and in his hand
Hold fast Ithuriel's spear, lest some foul toad
Inspire the restless mind with idle dreams,
Which better fit it for adulterous league
With Error than the sober walks of Truth.
Yet he that would esteem himself a man,
Should probe each honest question of his time,
And having two eyes, keep them both alert,
One in the search of truth and one of shadows,
And, proving all things, hold fast what is good."

"Or bide his time for such developments
As will endow his faculties to act
With the precision of intelligence.
Danger runs hand in hand with Haste. When ripe,
Truth falls of its own weight, and sinks at once
Into the soil of conscience, bringing forth
Fruit of its kind; plucked green, it quickly rots
And fails an issue. What if those who seem
Angels of light—if they be more than shadows
From fever-warmed imagination cast
Upon the screen of some unfathomed power
Of intellect—rather prove enemies
Of human peace and happiness, whose light
Is darkness, or the stolen robes of Truth
In which, as in sheep's clothing, they essay
Lawless approach to this unsheltered fold,
And stealing in with serpent subtlety,
And ready counterfeit of friendship's voice,
Feed open-mouthed Credulity with lies
Fatal to order, peace and innocence?"

"It were not strange if from the vast Unseen,
Where the prolific broods of Life and Death
Are gathered, spirits of all mind should rush
Toward the back-opening doorway of the Earth,
Or its breached wall, if haply they may gain
The ear of student or companion fond,
In which to pour the stream of burning knowledge
Hard to retain so long. Nor doth the mind
Of devil less than angel yearn to sow

Its seed in kindred soil. The cormorant,
As well as dove, delights to propagate
Its carrion-loving race. Thus, unrestrained
By conscience, disembodied fools or knaves
May oft push honest folk aside, and seize
The disappointed ear of those who sit
In this half-lighted auditorium,
Or hold high carnival with kindred spirits.
For this good reason, possibly, the sky-lights
Were barred of old, and may again be closed
Till better order is obtained—the more
As those whose chaste attention would invite
A better class of speakers blush at note
Of any impropriety or lie,
And leave the court-room as a place unfit
For Christians; so the devil's witnesses
And lawyers have it their own way,—and will
Till modest people dare to brave the fight,
And brand the tongue of falsehood, whether clothed
In flesh, or wind-blown clouds of noxious vapor,—
Learning at length through sore experience
How to distinguish between foe and friend,
By inward rather than external signs,—
And that the law of progress does not end
With this primary school, this nursery
Of character and wisdom, but holds good
Even to the highest university,
Where the archangels teach God's mysteries
To the celestial savans and bright ranks
Of knowledge-loving cherubim, and turn,

Not seldom, to their reverend President
For counsel and instruction. Till mankind,
Emancipated by the Inward Light,
Have learned the conjoint use of faith and reason,
The world is ill equipped for its advancement
Into the higher walks of liberty,
Where Truth and Error, Light and Darkness still
Debate the empire of the mind. I doubt not
Even the van of Freedom's toiling host,
As oft before, will turn from Canaan's shores,
To wander in the wilderness of doubt
And fruitless controversy, until Death
Relieves the world of yet another race."

" Methinks their flight is not without excuse ;
For, first, they are not well assured that Moses
Hath ordered this advance, but the reverse ;
And, secondly, of all the prudent spies
They have sent forward, ten in every twelve
Have not obtained the vintage of En-gedi,
But a mere milk and honey beverage,
More fitted for the sick and sorrowing,
Than for the diet of inquiring minds,—
And have indeed seen giants, somewhat spectral
Perhaps, but of a most pretentious bearing,
And hostile to those claims by Christians held,
To whose encounter they are loth to bring
The tender wisdom of their little ones,
Though for themselves they might not shun the assault.
And surely, from the sum of evidence

Thus far obtained,—if aught thereof be real—
We must conclude that many in those regions
Are such as were more wisely shunned than courted."

"And for these reasons men will turn away
From the apparent proof and demonstration
Of immortality, which unto some
Are sweeter than the purple wealth of Eschol,
And worth a journey o'er the Border-lands
Of Time to gain, though but a single cluster,
With toil and weariness, could be brought back,
Suspended on a stick between men's shoulders!
But those whose eyes are always backward turned,
To find a warrant for their Christ-bought freedom
In the example of Earth's twilight ages,
Will ever bow before a Golden Calf,
And fly affrighted from each show of danger."

"The votaries of this apocalypse
Seem quite as likely to bestow their worship
On a poor Golden Calf, as those who trust
In proofs which have endured the rack and strain
Of twenty centuries. In dignity,
In calm intensity of moral power,
In godlike purpose and consistency,
In grand effect, how far do those excel
These puny miracles of modern time!
Yet men will bow before a dancing stick,
And with wide-throated confidence imbibe
The silly drivel of a sorcerer,

Who stand unmoved before the glorious life
And solid wisdom of the Son of God."

"Which, though irrational, should point the wise
To one of nature's laws. A tallow candle
At hand out-shines the distant Pleiades!
A summer novel will attract more readers,
To spend the midnight oil upon its pages,
Than the Old Romance of a dying World,
Saved by the blood of her Celestial Lover!—
Observing which, some of the star-eyed muses
Have lately turned their wits to novel writing,
And thereby, through an art long time tabooed
By such as praised the sacred parables,
Rendered effective service to the cause
Of piety and virtue. Better thus
To cleanse all channels of intelligence
And rational delight, than weakly yield
To thieves the fairest province of Truth's realm."

"But tell me now, are not these modern dreamers
More given to their idols than the zealot,
Who, in his darkened cloister, counts his beads,
Or conjures with his relic, fancying
The saints will hold to him by their attachment
To cast-off clothes? Nay, are not the sincere
And the enlightened, who perhaps may find
Some grains of truth among the sands of folly,
And sometimes feel the heart-beat of the angels,
Or through their own, or through another's pulses,

In danger of transferring unto these,
The homage and attention due to God?
Gravely I question whether wise or weak
Would much advantage gain from laying bare
Those secrets unto which an inborn faith
Has thus far been the key, sufficient found
By all who trust in God, to nourish hope
And strengthen virtue for more solid growth
Than might arise from grounds of certainty.
What if the clouds which brood above our heads,
Reflecting or restraining heaven's pure light,
Could be, by more than Fancy's eye, transformed
To angel, human, or demoniac faces,
Lustrous or dark, such as the dreaming boy
Can see in every rack,—how could our thoughts
Go through them up to God, or Love its way
Find mid the radiant throng of witnesses
That hover round the earth,—did they not veil
Their heart-entangling beauty to protect
Our innocent devotions—how, I say,
Could Love the pathway to its Father find?"

"Precisely as it does in Earth or Heaven,
Once having learned the art of social praise,
And what the Word of Faith long since declared
Of God's true dwelling-place,—nor up, nor down,
But in the loving heart and truthful lips.
Yet I confess to no small peril here,
For that prime root of woe, Idolatry,
Doth so impinge upon the Tree of Life,

That in man's heart their branches interlace,
And not unfrequently a mongrel growth
Of piety engender, very grievous
To the Good Father. For this cause, perhaps,
When man became infatuate for knowledge
Of things beyond his years, God drew a veil
Before the heavens, lest by an outward glory
Rather than moral excellence, his heart
Should be engaged. But when redeeming grace
Had again planted in his soul the germs
Of piety and wisdom, and good root
Therefor obtained, it pleased the Viewless One
To set before the hungry eyes of men
An Image of His person, dim at first,
Of purpose to make inward worth more winning,
And separate the dross from faith's true gold;
But presently outrivaling the sun,
In the pure splendors of that glorious Form,
In which, to make his triumph over Sin
And Death complete, the Son of God appeared
Not once, but many times to those who loved him,
And could the vision bear. Herein perchance
He did not fail to set a safe example
To such as could obey it, for his angels
Did oft succeed in breaking through the mists
Of physical impurity, which cloud
Man's spiritual sight, and to the prophets—
A most prolific household in those times—
In diverse ways communicate their thoughts,
Which burned for utterance, so that, while one

Was speaking through his medium, another
Would suddenly break out, incompetent
To hold the fiery beam which through him shot
From Truth's warm-shining Sun. And so it came
That frequently confusion took the place
Of order, such a crowd of spirits yearned
To add their voices to the swelling chorus
Of immortality: and some for Christ,
And some for Antichrist their voices raised,
Causing the wise apostles to lay down
Rules for their government, and for the trial
Of those who spoke, holding the spirits subject
Unto the prophets, and excluding those
Who testified against the Truth. All this
Under the eyes of those clear-sighted bishops,
Which the Lord set to guard his infant fold,
For many years transpired. Nor was it wisdom,
Virtue, or heaven-imposed necessity,
But rather human weakness, ever prone
To change God's richest blessings to a curse,
Which caused the groaning gates of Paradise
To close once more over a darkening world,
Thenceforth for dreary centuries, a prey
And sporting-ground for devils, who, like wolves
In sheep's attire, ravaged the bloody fold,
And drove the frantic and disheveled Church,
Again into the Wilderness, where God
Her secret place prepared, and there has fed her,
Well nigh her two and forty months, with bread
Of faith, by unseen fingers scattered round

Her melancholy camp. But she begins
Once more to hunger for a change of diet
And open vision of that Heavenly Country,
Which is her fit inheritance. What think you?
Is it more Christ-like to submit to wrong,
Or drive out evil with the rod of Truth?"

"Both that and this, as ordered in God's time.
Perhaps where dangers compass every walk,
He will best reach his goal who in tried paths
Directs his steps, not emulous to gain
Wealth by uncertain ventures, while enough
Is given for each day's uses."
                              "O, my friend!
Thou hast not parted with the half thy soul!
It may be well for those who feel no lack
To rest in their contentment, until God
Moves them to keen inquiry if the heavens
Must needs be ever silent, silent, silent,
To love's importunate appeal! The World
Has not outgrown the need of restless hearts,
Ready to do and dare in Love's sweet service;
Or curious explorers bent to find
Each crevice in her golden hills. E'en Caution
Is not at all times prudent. Those whom men
Call mad are the World's saviours : martyr-like,
They fling contempt upon the World's cold wisdom,
And, fired by some great master passion, rush
Through Hell and death to immortality.
Cold Science doth not lack such votaries,

Willing to forfeit life for but a taste
Of Nilus' fountain, or one happy glance
At the Earth's bare and frozen axis. Lo!
How rival nations squander wealth and tears
To win a glacier, while, just above them,
The green and argent fields of Paradise
Wave welcome from innumerable homes
Of love and light—all vainly wave, to gain
But an indifferent or scornful glance
From those who deem life honorably spent
In wresting from the Earth's reluctant bosom,
Or close-mouthed skies, their secrets. While with lens
And spectroscope man conjures with the stars,
And makes continuous inroads upon heaven,
Wooing the spirits of the vasty deep
To own us for their kindred, shall no charm
Of love, or irresistable wand of faith,
From the mind's inner constellations draw
Their heart-inspiring treasures? While from shore
To shore of Earth's long sundered continents
We send our greeting on the lightning's wing,
Bidding adieu to absence, time and space,
Shall that ethereal ocean, which divides
Life's widowed hemispheres, forevermore
Our arts defy? Shall Jordan's rivulet,
Which from the prophet's fallen mantle fled,
And from the Ark of God's redeeming love,
Be never bridged with golden strands of thought,
Though dark Niagara's chasm has been spanned?
O, shame! that men should be ashamed to ask,

With solemn earnestness, if there be found
At last a medium, however humble,
Whereby we can some tidings gain of those
Who drew our heart-strings with them when they went
Forth from our sighing tents, perhaps no farther
Than Canaan from that Border Land, whereto,
Their warfare done, a fifth of Israel's tribes
Did gain consent their loving steps to turn!
Pray whither should our wandering lovers stray,
To find a sweeter pasture than our thoughts
Awhile afford, till they grow brown and juiceless,
Because the heavens give down no freshening rain?
Should they go nibbling round other planets?
Or board some comet steaming o'er heaven's main,
And search for joy in fair celestial islands?
When far from home, and this maternal Orb
Whose eye still follows lovingly their flight,
Weary with sight of strangers and strange lands,
Will they not languish with sweet homesickness,
And say unto their Father, "Father, dear,
We long to see again our Mother's face,
And our sweet sisters and fond brothers kiss,
Tenderly—oh, so soft and tenderly
Upon their hearts, that they shall think of us,
And say, are not our heavenly loved ones near?"
Would not the Father to his oarsmen say,
'Turn thitherward your swift heaven-cleaving wings,
And take my darlings wheresoe'er they will?'"

"And when returned with so much freight of learning,
Methinks they should be able to augment
Somewhat our meagre stores. But what new truths
Has the world thus far gathered from these pale
And crossing meteors, which sometimes shower
Upon us from an unknown sphere ? We deem
The stars are falling, but when morning comes,
Nothing remains of all the fair display
But wonderment and dust ! " •
       "Yet thus may fall—
Mostly no doubt in inconspicuous rain,
With now and then a flash of angels' wings,—
The pollen which the conjugal Heavens bestow
To foster Earth's enlarging life, and give
To her crude growths that rising excellence
Which hints at contact with superior orbs.
Conjecture well may weary with surmising
Of all the possible benefits mankind
May gather from these ghostly visitants.
But if that one vast, hard, soul-buffeting question
Of Immortality could by these means
Be comfortably laid amid the tombs
Of old forgotten problems, who would not
Thank God, and enter on his proper work
With two-fold energy, striving to lay
The stones of his eternal habitation
In pleasant places ?"
      "Some might thus improve
Their firm assurance, others take new lease
Of self-indulgence, seeing life is long

And may have many turns—each one, of course,
As the fools always are, a vast improvement
On the preceding! But if so much good,
And chiefly good, can spring from these revealings—
These late-discovered oil-founts of the sky—
Why were they so long hidden from mankind?
Or, if not wholly to the past unknown,
Why was their use of old inhibited?
Why should God frown such blessings into darkness?"

"For the same reason that He veiled men's bodies
When Liberty with Innocence was slain,—
To guard them from temptation and excess,
And bound their passions by the law of love.
Their use for evil only was denied,
While freely to the honest prophets granted
Who in their schools had learned the needful art
Of winnowing the golden grain of truth
From its encumbering dust and chaff. The same
Wise limitation at this day is binding.
The sorcerer is but spiritual harlot
Who prostitutes Heaven's gifts for lust or gain,
And without sanctifying love disports
With life's profoundest sanctities. In part
To Nature due, in part to use, this power
Is a more sensuous development
Of that profound and wondrous womb of thought,
Imagination, common to the race,
But in the poet's mind preëminent—
So all alive to nature's sympathies,

And the complete analogies which form
The base of spiritual knowledge, that when the truth
Enters the mind there is at once conceived
A figurative form appropriate
To its peculiar features, form the germs
Of Nature's infinite correspondencies,
Cell-like, in memory stored. In common parlance,
The instruments of thought's embodiment
Are arbitrary types by art invented—
Symbols of earth or air where thought takes form
For observation, that it may project
And multiply itself in other minds.
But poets add to language picture types,
As artists do to books, making the germs
Of fancy blossom out before the eye.
Hence poets are twin-brothers of the prophets
In whom imaginative faculty
Projects its power into the nervous system,
And so endows it that when spirit forms
Are present, from the finer media
Of nature—the magnetic aura which invests
Our lower life, forming an atmosphere
For commerce and reflection between brain
And spirit—there is formed an auratype,
Or apparition of the ghostly presence,
Or such responsive motions as will signal
Its operations to ear, eye, or touch.
To what extent art may improve this rare
And wondrous faculty—no more divine

Than all God's gifts—and for our happiness,
Or higher growth employ it, time must prove.
Like all the kindred powers of soul and body,
Immensely competent for good or ill,
It should with love-bound continence be used—
Discreetly, reverently in virtue's service,
With due respect of Nature's just relations.
He who transforms a ghost into a god,
Or woes it but for idle dalliance,
Or seeks to harness it before his cart,
May find himself a ghost-bestridden fool,
Spurred swiftly into error's thorny paths.
But he that with a heart reposed on God,
And mind illumined by His secret beam,
Inquires what good, what truth, what joy of love,
What comfort of assurance may be found
In this or any door of being's wide
And various temple, though he may not find
All his desire, or meet at every turn
Truth-telling guides, yet, if he do respect
The laws of those dominions, and regard
The imperfections of his counsellors,
And the proprieties of time and place,
He shall not be repelled as an intruder,
But welcomed with a Father's gracious smile,
And by good angels helped along the dark
And stony paths of life, more cheerful made
By these faint glimpses of a better world."

THE MORNING STAR.

Welcome! welcome! sister dear,
  From the dark and stormy sea!
From the waves of doubt and fear,
  To the Home of Liberty!
Welcome to the House of Cheer,
  And our Happy Family!

Welcome to the peaceful Skies!
  All thy weary tasks are done!
Sister, lift thy drooping eyes,
  And behold our Chosen One!
Sorrow from His presence flies,
  Like the clouds before the Sun!

Doubt and sadness all are flown!
  Death has lost his mortal sting!
Love hath made us all his own
  By his patient suffering!
High upon his golden throne,
  Love in every heart is King!

Bowing meekly to the rod,
  Man's deliverance to gain,
Buried oft beneath the sod
  Of his sluggish heart and brain,
Worthy Son and Lamb of God,
  Take thy Father's might and reign!

VIII.

"PRAY hast thou thus heard aught from thy beloved,
Since o'er death's abrogated bourne she passed?"

"Such is my very pleasant confidence."

"By what sound tokens justified?"
"By proofs,
Intrinsic and extrinsic, such as wrought
Conviction in my willing mind."
"O'erwilling,
It may be, for the critical regard
Which such pretensions merit."
"Possibly;
And yet to ask for light, and straightway close
Our eyes to its appeal, if novel found,
Is little wiser than to credit things
Incredible, because we wish them true."

"Well, what good tidings did she bring—what truths
Of new and wondrous import—from the realms
Of pure celestial radiance?"

" Did Messias
Teach men new truths, or vitalize the old ones ?—
And how should babes excel the Lord's Anointed ?
Were they to startle us with prodigies
Beyond our power to image or conceive,
What profit would they gather from their tale ?"

"Well, what of cheer or comfort ?"
                    " Words of love,
That tasted of the virtues of my sister,
And helped me to conceive her living presence."

"Aught of advice or warning ?"
                    " Yes, these words,
"' Do not fear death, my brother.'"
                    "Did she speak
Of her demise, and tell you in what manner
Death handles us ?"
                    "She said, 'I seemed to sleep
A little while, then woke as from a dream—
So strange it seemed, that all which caused me pain
Was left.'"
          " Of the condition of her mind ?"

" That she remembered all I said to her—
Meaning the words of courage, which I spoke
In the last hours, saying a sweet surprise
Awaited her, to find how slight a change,
And yet how great death brings—that what we call
Death is but going up the river's bank,

In whose cold waters we so long have waded :—
Likewise, that she was happy and content."—

Did she assent that she had seen her Saviour,
Him, for whose love she said so touchingly
In her soul's widowhood, that she was willing
To go and agonize, even through death?"

"She did, and that He is the very Sun
Of that Celestial World where she is dwelling,
Whose beauty she could not describe."
       "Nor tell you
Of its location?"
    "It is both adjacent
To this dull orb, and at removes therefrom,—
Somewhat as it may please the immigrant
To pitch his tent, near or remote from kindred."

"'Tis very likely some would rest as well
At a good stone's-throw from their relatives—
Quite out of hearing of the whir and murmur
Of this ill-kept soul-factory, whose windows—
Stained with the sullen mixtures of the shop,
So they be scarcely more than half translucent—
Perhaps the idle boys are knocking in,
Rather than angels opening; and whose workmen,
Each on his wedding-robe or shroud engaged,
Are all so busy with their toils or gossip,
They seldom lift their eyes to see the angels,
Who bend so pityingly and fondly o'er them.

Or shall I rather name the Earth an iceberg,
On which the heavenly flocks may sometimes light,
But will full soon spread out their flashing pinions
To find a warmer perch?"
        "Nor may we blame them,
Since they could win no sign of recognition
From our dull organs. Yet they are not moved
By selfishness like men, but hover round,
As doth a mother-bird about her nest,
Eager to lodge a grain of heavenly truth
In our blind, gaping souls, still fondly hoping
That we shall finally behold their faces."

"Do they at all times thus invest us?"
          "No;—
Save that a subtle thread of consciousness
Attends them in their travels, not unlike
The gossamer, which prudent spiders leave
Behind them in their flights, or telegraph,
Which armies, those huge spiders, draw along,
In their marauding march. But these with love
Thus bridge their partial absence, and secure
A swift return if dangers call, or grief
Pull at their heart-strings. Rather, I might say,
To speak profoundly, God who is that Sea
Of spiritual fire, out of whom all things
Have sprung, and in whom they subsist, when moved
By our distress or want, as with a wave
Of light, or instant pulse of gravity,
Touches their hearts with sense of our desire,

And speeds them on the sunbeams of His love
To our relief."
    " Have they no dwelling-place,
No mansion in their Father's ample House,
Where kindred souls may twine congenial thoughts
About some darling interest, unstarred
By lesser loves?"
    "I asked my fair informant
If she had such a home to call her own;
And she replied, 'I have, a lovely one.'"

"Did you inquire its nature?"
        "Ah! my friend,
Such questions, born of curiosity
Rather than true heart-hunger, touching love,
Sometimes breed curious answers. If the wise
Are speaking, they may say they cannot tell:
But with a change of spirit in our minds,
The way is opened for a change without;
And while one hesitates, being unwilling
To give us disappointment or reproof,
Another from the crowd of witnesses,
Not all benign, around us, may breathe forth
Some vain conceit, or touch the soft antennæ
With which the spirit feels its way to knowledge,
As mischief-loving boys annoy the snail,
Slow journeying with his house upon his back,
To see him slink into his tortuous hall."

"Wherein, if this be true, does Heaven excel
This mocking world of sense, where Truth and Error
Play foot-ball with our minds, till nothing seems
Assured but doubt and ambiguity?
O how our spirits yearn for some abode,
Where nothing false or hurtful can invade!—
Where the wicked cease from troubling, and the weary
Find rest! But now these sad revealings come
To rob us of that hope, and make us doubt
If death than life be better! Were this gospel
Ordained of God, should it bring forth such fruits?"

Did that aforetime sent make peace or conflict
Its opening act? Dealt it with only men,
Or with the principalities and powers
Of populous Ether? What if the still haven
To life's tumultuous sea be in a heart
Centered on God, amid the bellowing storms
Of elemental havoc and disaster?
An outward peace may come, compatible
With inward harmony, time adequate
Being allowed for life's adjoining spheres,
To break the waves of conflict from below.
Such is, at least, our grateful theory
Of life, perhaps more puerile than fair:—
For who, like God, still battles with the might
Of fiercest Hell? or who, like Adam, feels
The sting of sin in his last grand-child's heart?
O'er ever-widening areas of light
With Christ to reign, is bliss enough for hope.

Heaven walks unharmed through subterranean fires,
And Hell through Eden's balmy fields unchanged."

"What final fortune waits those acrid spirits
Which not e'en death or sight of Heaven can purge
Of their deep-seated bitterness and woe?
Some light on this grave question should be shed
By these eye-witnesses of destiny."

"I asked a noble angel, and he said:
'They live forever.' Thereat being grieved,
Because I wished them dead or well-converted,
I spoke another, and he did confirm
That dread, and straitly charge that I teach
No other doctrine. Having still a doubt,—
So hard it is to give away our mind,
And judging that the spirit carries with it,
Full long, the firm opinions held in Earth,—
I asked my sister if she knew of any
Deemed wise in Heaven who held another view?
She said she did not, but would ascertain
If such there were, and give me information.
So after many days, when from my thoughts
The theme had passed, she came again and said:
'It is impossible for you to know
The final of the lost ones. We can give
Our thoughts, our best impressions of the truth;
But for the infinite and the eternal
God only is sufficient.' Then I ceased,
Feeling, in my own consciousness, that Truth
Had spoken."

"Does not the good Father speak
Distinctly, and allay His children's doubts?"

"God speaks in life and light, leaving our organs
To give embodiment unto His Word.
But, varying in their action, or impressed
With previous conceptions, these attribute
Diversity of feature and expression
To that which comes from God. What is essential
To our integrity and happiness
Is with all needful certainty defined;
And for the rest it harms not if we differ,
So Charity forget not her sweet office.
Both men and angels view the face of God,
In radiance of moral truths disclosed,
As loving students read the face of Nature,
Feeding on themes adapted to their taste,
And leaving somewhat for the morrow's study."

"What meanest thou by angels? Are there none
Of higher rank than such as once were men?"

"Three of the four to whom I put the question
Gave negative replies. The last, a spirit
Of loftiest inspiration in his youth,
Averred he had both seen and talked with such.

"From these successes it doth not appear
That all the books of Wisdom will be laid
Open to our inspection by this key,

Even if placed in wise and honest hands ;—
Perhaps but little more than could be read
By due attention to that subtle Beam
Which is not barred by flesh, but which informs
Alike both men and angels, making use
Of all the vast and wondrous artistry
Of Nature's intricate loom to shadow forth
The heavenly principles and substances
Which underlie the fabric of our visions.
A hint perhaps to help us in our musings,
A token of sweet sympathizing love,
A word of cheer, may sometimes be vouchsafed,
To break the weariness of death's long silence.
But chiefly through the normal avenues
Of thought and feeling, which should ever lie
Wide open upward, our celestial friends,
Should hold communion with us, satisfied
With that which God enjoys, and thus escape
The dangers and embarrassments which spring
From contact with life's lower elements.
Thus, like a pure transparent atmosphere
Surrounding this beclouded world of sense,
They may transmit the radiance of Heaven
Unto our souls, less colored by their own
Peculiar views,—thus in our joys rejoice,
And, with divine benignity, allay
Our sorrows, leaving all our members free
To do their proper work, unawed by weight
Of foreign power. This mortal still is weak,
And ill can bear the welding fires which knit
The golden links that bind the Earth to Heaven."

"My friend, thou speakest with the subtlety
Of one that has seen sorrow and has walked
With Disappointment, arm in arm, and watched
Her shadowy finger, as with solemn mien,
She points to Wisdom's low but fruitful path,
And to the hem of that celestial robe
Whose Wearer, from the pressure of our wants
And our infirmities, we cannot reach.
Touch it and be content, and from thy soul
The wasting flow, the mining wretchedness,
May cease, and joy and thanks to Heaven ascend,
A sweeter sacrifice than useless grief.
The sum of that which I propound is this,
That man, as God's true child, by Nature first
And afterwards by grace, is made joint heir
With Christ of being's two-fold, wedded realm;
To which inheritance he will arrive
At his majority, when Heavenly Truth,
Ascending and descending on the Earth
By every round of progress fairly won,
Has made him free indeed. "All things to me
Are lawful," said the noble citizen
Both of Jerusalem and Rome. To this
High standard we are called—by Reason's light,
And that diviner Beam which doth inform
Reason and conscience, acting on the words
Spoken of God, and all the gathered mass
Of man's experience, to prove all things,
And hold fast the expedient, the good.
Then from thought's radiant summits we may see

Jerusalem descending as a bride
From Heaven, adorned to meet her Lord ; then join
The universal anthem of her saints,
Rolling from land to land from sphere to sphere :—
"Maker of all things and Thyself the bond
Invisible between life's various ranks,
We crown Thee Lord of being's boundless Realm !
From Earth's rich harvest-fields and Heaven's bright
    bowers,
No longer severed by the ocean widths
Of death, we lift accordant songs of praise,
Triumphing in His might beneath whose feet
Error and wrong lie crushed, while nations rise
Emancipated from the servile yoke
Of ignorance and sin ! Hail radiant Sun
Of Righteousness and Truth ! breaking at last
In glory through the morning shades, to give
Peace, light and freedom to a ransomed World !
Sole Heir of the eternities ! of God
Only Begotten ! to Thy rightful sway
All things at last shall bow in Earth and Heaven !
Death owns Thee King ! the Grave acknowledges
Thy sovereignty and her vast plunder yields
To swell the glory of Thy conquering train,
As with archangels and the countless host
Of Thy Celestial Empire Thou again
Dost pay mankind divine respect—not now
In sorrow and humility to plead
With a rebellious and unthankful race,
But as Bridegroom hastening to his Bride,

Thou ridest through the purple gates of morn,
In chariot of gold with sapphires crowned,
Gathering night's jewels, like golden sheaf,
Into thy bosom—STAR OF MORNING Thou,
And of the Day, Immortal Son of God!"

When Soul is sick and Heart is sad
   And spirits go a-sighing;
When Hope is blind and Reason mad
   And Fear and Doubt are lying;
And Love a-swooning o'er the tomb
   Can neither sleep nor waken,
O what can make the cyprus bloom,
   Or heal the hearth forsaken?

Let Nature pour her softest balms
   And tune her sweetest voices;
Let Ocean chant his grandest psalms
   Till every isle rejoices;
Let meadows bloom and orchards blush;
   Let Earth deck all her daughters;
Let fountains leap and torrents rush
   With joy of living waters;

Let Day and Night in festive mood
   Pour out their richest treasures,
And sight and science fire the blood
   With their amazing measures;—
And is the heart by these made whole,
   That hath no heart within it?

O, soulless Heart! O, heartless Soul!
    Joy withers ere I win it!

Go forth and join the manly strife
    Where passion grandly blazes!
Let action swell the stream of life,
    And sweep its stagnant mazes!
Rock out thy spirit's bitterness
    On life's tumultuous ocean,
And quench its void and vain distress
    With power's sublime emotion!

Where wreath or crown with silvery light
    On every hill is shining,
And hopes attained new hopes incite,
    O, who should sit repining?
There's joy in action, storm and haste,
    In gaining and in giving!
And if one blossom is laid waste,
    There still are many living!—

Alas! alas! the soul is deep,—
    So nought but God is deeper!
When Peace and Joy there fall asleep
    Can conflict wake the sleeper?
The World may fret, or smile, or foam,—
    'Tis but a traveler's story!—
The heart which keeps its fire at home
    Alone finds rest and glory!

Then inward, inward turn for might!
  Below thy deepest sorrow
There is a Fountain filled with light,
  Where sleeps a fair to-morrow!
Earth may not bid that morrow live,
  Or still thy bosom's yearning;
But He who built love's fire can give
  The fuel to its burning!

If on the wreck of mortal good
  Thy thoughts in darkness ponder;
If o'er death's awful solitude
  Thy fainting spirit wander;
Crushed by thy burden to the sod,
  Led like the lamb to slaughter,
Still nearer press thy soul on God,
  For THERE *is living water!*

Since Sin unlocked the door of Death,
  And plumed his somber pinion,
Each flake that floats on Time's cold breath,
  Must own his pale dominion;
But since the Lord on Calvary
  Repulsed his fiercest dashes,
Through mourning flows the oil of joy,
  And beauty springs from ashes!

O, Heart and Hope! then bide your time!
  There is a season waiting,
When Life, returning to her prime,

Shall feel no more abating ;
When He who lets the tear-tides flow,
Will bid joy's currents chase them,
And all your jewels missed below,
Above ye shall embrace them !

For Love He is the King of kings !
The Soul's delightful Lover !
And all who hide beneath His wings,
He will from grief recover !
And he whose faith, mid drought and gloom,
Still roots in truth and duty,
Shall crown his brow with Eden's bloom,
And kiss the King of Beauty !

And as He bends His glory down,
To smile away our sadness,
The stars that glimmer in His crown
Shall twinkle forth their gladness,
And whisper from their bowers above,
" Rejoice ! To Love is given
The victory !—for God is Love,
And Love is Home and Heaven !"

www.ingramcontent.com/pod-product-compliance
Lightning Source LLC
Chambersburg PA
CBHW030356170426
43202CB00010B/1395